MW01166576

"A true love of radio and unwavering determination were the fuel that launched Shotgun Tom on a rocket ship ride to the 'bigs'. Add nonstop energy and the heart of an entertainer and you have Shotgun's recipe for success. Better believe it, baby."

– Charlie Van Dyke, legendary Top 40 DJ

"Shotgun Tom isn't just a legendary and phenomenal radio personality. He is the guy next door, the one with the model trains, the one with the cool hat, the one who loves his family – his listeners – his life! With this book, we all get to know the WHOLE story about one of the most enduring voices in radio history. Like my mom used to say, 'It's nice to be important, but it's more important to be nice'. Shotgun checks off both boxes big time!"

– Lou Simon, VP/Music Programming,
SiriusXM Radio

"Shotgun is what a radio DJ should be: entertaining, energy and lots of warmth to project on the air. He has been so consistent over the years. Every day is powerful and entertaining radio, as it should be. He is one of the best jocks I ever have worked with."

– Dan Mason, Former President,
CBS Radio, New York

"Shotgun was a dream to work with. He showed up every day with the same enthusiasm. He was always well prepared and contemporary. Shotgun is a big personality, not just a big voice."

– Pat Duffy, Vice President and General Manager,
CBS Radio's K-Earth 101 Los Angeles

All I Wanna Do Is Play The Hits!

All I Wanna Do Is Play The Hits!

Shotgun
Tom Kelly

with
Neil Ross

JCH Media
Publishing
Carlsbad, CA

Copyright © 2024 by Thomas Irwin

All rights reserved. No part of this publication may be reproduced, distributed, or transmitted in any form or by any means, including photocopying, recording, or other electronic or mechanical methods, without the prior written permission of the publisher, except in the case of brief quotations embodies in critical reviews and certain other noncommercial uses permitted by copyright law. For permission requests, write to the publisher, address "Attention: Permissions Coordinator," at the address below.

JCH»MEDIA PUBLISHING

JCH Media Inc.
3988 Monroe Street, Carlsbad, California 92008

Library of Congress Cataloging-in-Publication Data
has been applied for.

FIRST EDITION

ISBN: 979-8-9908956-0-7

Ordering information:
Special discounts are available on quantity purchases by corporations, associations, and others. For details, email tkarnold@jchmediainc.com.

JCH hardcover edition / July 2024
Printed in the United States of America

Production work by Write Away Books
Cover photo by Bob Freeman
Cover design by Beth Hutchins
Book Design: Gritton Design

This book is dedicated to my family:
My wife Linda; my daughter Melanie; and my son Nick

About Those QR Codes

To really make Shotgun Tom Kelly come alive, we've added QR codes throughout this book that will take you to some pretty cool video clips, including the Hollywood Walk of Fame ceremony in which Shotgun got his very own star; a 1972 documentary film on Shotgun's typical workday at KGB; a news report on Shotgun's model train layout; and other interesting moments in Shotgun's life.

To make them work, open the camera app on your smart phone, hover over the QR code, and then click on the highlighted link. It will take you straight to the video!

Foreword

For me and the many millions of other young people who grew up in the Sixties and Seventies, DJs were our larger-than-life heroes and our closest friends.

Rock 'n' roll was young, and in those glorious days before satellites and streaming transformed how we watch and listen to programs, radio was it. Radio brought rock 'n' roll into our homes, courtesy of those irrepressible Top 40 DJs who joked with us, laughed with us, talked with us and brought us the songs that would comprise the soundtracks to our young lives.

How many teenagers would plop themselves onto their beds after school and crank up the radio, closing their eyes as legendary DJs with names like Cousin Brucie, Wolfman Jack, The Real Don Steele and Shotgun Tom Kelly entertained us for hours with witty repartee before, after and sometimes during those marvelous, magical hits you only heard on the radio.

Shotgun Tom was one of the last big Top 40 DJs – or, as they are more properly known, radio personalities.

A bear of a man instantly identifiable by his trademark ranger hat and brrrrrr-yah sign-on, he probably had a bigger impact on Southern California teens in those golden days of rock 'n' roll than anyone.

He began his radio reign in San Diego, on AM powerhouses KCBQ and "Boss Radio" KGB, and later moved on to

B-100 when Top 40 radio migrated to FM. When the format splintered into more specialized formats, Shotgun Tom moved up to Los Angeles and kept the spirit of Top 40 radio alive for another two decades on the mighty oldies station KRTH. His popularity was such that in 2013, he was awarded a star on the prestigious Hollywood Walk of Fame, in a ceremony where he was introduced by none other than one of the greatest musicians of the past century, Stevie Wonder. He's still going strong to this day, reaching a national audience via satellite on his SiriusXM Sixties Gold Channel 73 radio show.

This book is a compelling account of Shotgun Tom's life and career, in his own words. We meet Tom as a young boy already obsessed with radio, telling a formidable parochial schoolteacher in no uncertain terms exactly what he wants to do with the rest of his life.

We watch Tom's obsession build as he sets up his own little radio station in his bedroom and heads downtown, where the DJs from his favorite station, KCBQ, broadcast from behind a huge glass window visible to everyone on the sidewalk below. We follow Tom as he gets his first radio job when he was just 16 years old and then pays his small-market dues before returning home to San Diego, where he rapidly ascends up the ranks of radio royalty.

We bear witness to the roller-coaster ride every DJ must contend with, where you're a star one day and fired the next. Shotgun Tom also opens up about some of the dark moments of his life, including his battle against drug addiction and major heart surgery that saved his life.

Shotgun Tom's story is one of perseverance, luck, and

redemption, as seen through the eyes of a man whose entire being was driven by a desire to play the hits – which he did, and is still doing today.

I was 13 when I discovered both radio and rock 'n' roll, a one-two punch that changed my life forever. Shotgun Tom's was the first voice I heard, and I was hooked, listening to him on my round, green Panasonic Panapet transistor radio pretty much all my waking hours.

One evening I was in the bathtub, listening to Shotgun Tom, when I heard the "Name It and Claim It" jingle followed by Shotgun's pronouncement that the sixth caller would win the record he had just played, provided, of course, that the caller correctly identified the song. "MacArthur Park!" I screamed to no one as I sprang from the tub, naked and wet, and ran to the kitchen to grab the phone.

This wasn't my first rodeo, but on all my previous tries, I either got a busy signal or I wasn't the correct caller. Imagine my surprise when the phone at the radio station picked up and I heard Shotgun Tom himself say, "Congratulations! You're the sixth caller! Can you name it and claim it?" I could, and I did.

The next day, my mom drove me to KGB's studio off Pacific Highway and I picked up my prize: a seven-inch 45 of Richard Harris singing "MacArthur Park."

Yeah, I know. The song wasn't my cup of tea, either. But I had won it on the air from Shotgun Tom Kelly himself, and I treasured that little single as though it was solid gold. I still have it.

A few weeks later, I heard on the radio that Shotgun was

going to be at the San Diego Wild Animal Park. I begged my parents to take me, which they did. They couldn't understand why I had absolutely zero interest in the animals. All I cared about was seeing Shotgun Tom.

My childhood hero eventually became my friend. I grew up and became a journalist, covering radio for *Billboard*, the *Los Angeles Times* and *San Diego Magazine*. Now Shotgun Tom and I were running in the same circles. We even judged a few Halloween contests together.

We lost touch when I took a job in Orange County and settled in North County to raise a family, only to reconnect years later when my kids had grown and I finally had time to rekindle old friendships. I started attending his Saturday night "pool hall" gatherings, which you'll read about in this book, and even brought along one of my sons to join in the fun.

Whenever I'm over there at Shotgun's house, either playing pool, chatting with other radio veterans in the broadcast studio he's set up in his home, or watching him man his elaborate model train layout that is suspended over his pool table, I think back to that little kid in the bathtub and the thrill I got from winning a vinyl record of "MacArthur Park."

At that moment, as I look over at Shotgun Tom Kelly holding court among his friends and fans, there's not a single place in the whole wide world I'd rather be.

— Thomas K. Arnold
July 2024

Table of Contents

Tom, You're A Star!

It was April 30, 2013. I'd been preparing for this moment for years, since I was 10, although back then I could never have imagined it. This was the morning I was going to be awarded a star on the Hollywood Walk of Fame!

The Hollywood Walk of Fame is a historic landmark consisting of nearly 3,000 terrazzo-and-brass stars embedded in the sidewalks along 15 blocks of Hollywood Boulevard and three blocks of Vine Street.

They are monuments to the biggest stars in entertainment. Many of my childhood heroes are immortalized here: Broderick Crawford, David Janssen, Johnny Mathis, Stevie Wonder....

And now so am I!

My Hollywood Walk of Fame experience began the morning of June 22, 2012, the day I logged onto the website to find out who would receive a Hollywood Walk of Fame star the following year. I had been nominated twice before, but never made the cut. On this day, I was fully prepared to once again be let down when much to my surprise, and delight, actress Marg Helgenberger announced my name!

I was blown away. Later on that magical day, KNX AM Newsradio's highly respected afternoon anchor, Diane Thompson, interviewed me live on the air.

Ten months later, the night before the awards ceremony, I rehearsed my acceptance speech, written by Hollywood TV and movie scribe Ken Levine. My wife, daughter and longtime friend and radio historian Art Vuolo Jr. were my captive audience as I rehearsed countless times.

My Hollywood director friend, Alan Brent Connell, was busy recording all the news coverage for me that morning. Alan was also busy with his camera and would take some outstanding photos at the ceremony. He later presented me with a phenomenal book of photos depicting every moment of my day.

My out-of-town friends and my son, Nick, and his friends were staying at the historic Hollywood Roosevelt hotel on Hollywood Boulevard. My wife and daughter, Melanie, were rooming with me in my apartment at Park La Brea.

As we woke up that morning, I was nervous, but I felt good about my speech and was ready to go as we awaited the limo. Right on time it pulled up, and we all piled in and made our way down La Brea Avenue to Hollywood Boulevard.

Meanwhile, my best friend, Tony Pepper, who was on his way

to the ceremony, called to say he was having trouble getting there because of heavy traffic.

"What the heck is going on, what is causing this traffic jam?" Suddenly he realized the traffic was caused by the hundreds of fans trying to get to my ceremony. "What's causing this traffic jam? It's you, Tom – you're a star!"

He wasn't wrong. At the event, my brother-in-law, Richard Brockman, who had flown in from Alabama, called my wife Linda to report, "Holy cow, Linnie, you will not believe the enormous crowd here for Tommy's big day!"

As we pulled up in the limo we could hear the Hollywood High School band practicing "Hooray for Hollywood," which they were scheduled to play at my ceremony. It was surreal to hear the band and watch the crowd assemble for my big moment.

I was filled with adrenaline. I found it hard to believe this was actually happening.

The limo dropped us off two blocks away from the ceremony site. As we walked up Hollywood Boulevard, we saw TV personality Josh Rubenstein and some fans gathered around the CBS 2 weather van. Josh suddenly asked me to join him as

Watch Josh Rubenstein's coverage by Alan Brent Connell and his wife Joanna of Shotgun Tom's Star ceremony.

he did his live weather report. I happily obliged!

George Pennacchio, Los Angeles entertainment reporter for KABC-7 Eyewitness News, was at CBS Television City covering "Dancing With the Stars." So, in order not to miss the star ceremony, he sent his video crew to Hollywood Boulevard to capture the moment, and he broadcast the report while covering "Dancing With the Stars." When he was finished, he placed one of my ranger hats on his head.

The late Sam Rubin, the Los Angeles entertainment reporter for KTLA TV Channel 5, promoted my ceremony on the morning of the event. It was great to have him promote the Star and encourage the Los Angeles audience to come to cheer me on.

In addition, KNX AM Newsradio anchor Dick Helton had me on his morning news show, along with Gary Bryan and Lisa Stanley from my radio station KRTH-FM.

Even my hometown San Diego TV station, KFMB-TV, sent their news anchor, Phil Blauer, to do a report on my star ceremony. I was touched that my hometown still thought so much of me to send their anchor to Hollywood to cover my big day.

Watch a video of KFMB-TV's San Diego news coverage of Shotgun Tom's Star ceremony.

As I made my way up to the location, I saw so many of my friends and family members. Among them I spotted Jeff Prescott, "Little Tommy" Sablan, Dave Sniff, my cousins the Whittaker family, and Jerry and Janet Klein, who owned A Better Deal Suits and Tuxedo Store.

Oh yes – they also provided me with the beautiful suit and tie you see on the cover of this book.

When I arrived, I passed Johnny Mathis and Stevie Wonder. Stevie was going to speak that day, along with KRTH program director Jhani Kaye. Seeing them and all the fans that had gathered filled me with so much emotion that without even thinking about it, I walked right over to a crowd of fans and started shaking their hands. "What a great idea -- who told you to do that?" Linda asked.

"It was an instant impulse to welcome all my fans who took time out of their day just for me," I said. I felt humbled beyond words.

Dan Mason, the president of CBS Radio, had the idea of giving away replicas of my trademark "Shotgun Tom" ranger hats and star pin on KRTH in the days preceding the event.

He figured the winners would show up to the ceremony wearing the hats. Dan was right! Looking over the crowd, there was a sea of "Shotgun Tom" ranger hats. Meanwhile, CBS Radio promotion director Patty Paster was coordinating the ceremony, along with the Hollywood Chamber of Commerce. Leron Gubler, president of the Hollywood Chamber of Commerce, was the master of ceremonies.

Leron welcomed everybody and read a glowing history

of how my career started and how a chance remark by my mother, LaVon Irwin, and a bicycle ride to a shopping center set the course for the rest of my life and career.

He welcomed up the first speaker, Jhani Kaye, who told the story of when I was chosen to be the first person in the world to play the brand-new John Lennon song, "Imagine," on KCBQ in San Diego in 1971 and made a mistake that still makes me cringe to this day. (We'll get into that later).

The next speaker was my longtime friend Stevie Wonder. Following his speech, Stevie suggested that he sing one of his songs for the crowd. Everyone was thrilled and began clapping. Then Stevie began singing "My Cherie Amour."

To the delight of the crowd, he changed the wording to: "Shotgun Tom Kelly, we listen to you on the radio."

Then it was my turn to speak. I stepped up and read the excellent speech that Ken Levine had written for me. Ken's a real pro and thanks to him, I received lots of claps and laughs. However, the last sentence of my speech was all mine. I wrote, and then said, "Ladies and gentlemen, as you walk over to my star here on Hollywood Boulevard, please curb your dog!"

With that, the star was unveiled.

The star recipient is responsible for throwing an after party at a "Hollywood" venue of their choice. I was extremely fortunate to have KRTH account executive Pam Baker arrange this big undertaking.

Pam was able to book the Hollywood Madam Tussauds Wax

Photo by Bob Freeman

Posing for the press.

Photo by Joanna Morones

Photo by Bob Freeman

Helping out with the installation of the star.

Photo by Alan Brent Connell

Meeting the fans.

Photo by Bob Freeman

Shotgun Tom and Stevie Wonder.

Photo by Bob Freeman

Melanie, Shotgun Tom, Linda and Nick Irwin.

Photo by Bob Freeman

Hundreds of people turned out for the April 30, 2013 ceremony.

Photo by Bob Freeman

Hey, I'm a star!

Museum roof-top patio for the party. It wasn't far from the ceremony. She was also instrumental in getting us a fantastic deal with Gloria Pink and her husband, owners of the iconic Pink's Hot Dog stand on La Brea Avenue.

Midway through the party, Mary Ayala, program director of San Diego news-talk radio station KOGO AM, called Linda and asked if I was available to be interviewed by Sully - the afternoon talk show host. I was very excited to be able to share my Hollywood Star experience with the San Diego audience.

The party turned into a fabulous extension of the ceremony. We had lots of friends and many of our family members in attendance. Stevie surprised us when he took time from his busy schedule to attend the party and be on hand for the many selfies everyone was clamoring for. It was the perfect venue with great food and celebrities, so Hollywood!

What a phenomenal day! Later, with watery eyes and a very full heart, I found myself thinking about how amazing it was that a kid from a sleepy San Diego suburb could find himself with a star at the place where the most legendary names in show business history are honored. It had been, indeed, as the Beatles might put it, a long and winding road. The story of that journey follows.

YOU should come visit.

Shotgun Tom's Star is at 7080 Hollywood Blvd., on the corner of La Brea and Hollywood Boulevard, right next to the legendary DJ The Real Don Steele.

Photo by Bob Freeman

The official kneeling shot!

Front row, L-R, Hollywood Walk of Fame chairman David Green, Shotgun Tom, Hollywood Chamber of Commerce president Leron Gubler. Back row, L-R, Stevie Wonder and Jhani Kaye.

Watch a video of Shotgun Tom's Star ceremony, including Stevie Wonder.

Let Me Tell You Something, Sister!

I knew what I wanted to do with my life when I was 10. At that age, some kids don't have a clue; some kids think they know and end up picking something else when the time comes.

But I knew at 10. I even remember the first time I actually put it into words.

I was a student at Saint John of the Cross Catholic school in San Diego. One day, during recess, I looked up and saw Sister Mario headed in my direction.

Sister Mario was a force to be reckoned with; just picture Kathleen Freeman as Sister Mary Stigmata, "The Penguin," in *The Blues Brothers* movie. She'd obviously taken note of my poor performance in school and had decided to do something about it.

Glaring down at me, she said, "Thomas! You must learn to read and spell and how to write a sentence and form a paragraph. You must learn these things to get along in life!"

I don't know what got into me, but I suddenly got angry. And as the anger welled up inside me, I looked her right in the eye and said, "Let me tell you something, Sister, ALL I WANNA DO IS PLAY THE HITS!"

What happened next is a little hazy, but it wasn't pleasant, as you might imagine. And, of course, Sister Mario was right. Everybody needs to know how to express themselves, vocally and on the page.

Basic math skills are important, too, along with some knowledge of geography, history and civics. Everyone in the modern world needs that kind of foundation – even the ones who "play the hits."

Eventually, I acquired those skills. Maybe not enough to satisfy Sister Mario, but enough to get me through life.

But I was right, too. All I wanted to do was become a radio DJ and play the hits. It's all I've ever wanted to do. I'm still doing it right up to this moment. I've loved every second of it. I've had a ball! My radio career has given me a lot of amazing adventures.

Now, I'd really like to tell you the story.

Beginnings

I was born in San Diego, California, on August 8, 1949 to John G. Irwin Sr. and LaVon Irwin.

My mom and dad had lived in Alliance, Nebraska, a small town in the western part of the state and the county seat of Box Butte County.

My dad, during the early years of his life, worked on the CB and Q (Chicago, Burlington and Quincy) Railroad. He started shoveling coal into the engine when he was 16. My mom went to nursing school at Saint Agnes Academy in Lincoln, Nebraska, and became a registered nurse.

John and LaVon met at a dance where my dad played drums in the orchestra. All the girls loved the guys in the band. (Girls and musicians, some things never change).

Up on the bandstand, my dad noticed my mom, managed to introduce himself and they started dating. They found out they had a lot in common.

One thing led to another, and they decided to get married and start a family.

The first child born in my family was my brother, John Gregory Irwin Jr. Around that time, my dad was promoted to Railroad Engineer on the CB and Q Railroad. While writing this chapter, I realize my dad worked for the CB and Q railroad and later in life I worked for KCBQ in San Diego. Odd coincidence.

As the family grew, another boy was born. They named him Robert. My mom decided to quit her job as a nurse in the hospital and stay home to take care of her growing brood. Mom, Dad, Greg and Bob continued to live in Nebraska for a couple more years. But, with Nebraska weather getting colder and colder, my parents started to look at places with warmer weather. In 1945, my parents and both of their families decided to move west to California.

My dad applied for a transfer to the Santa Fe railroad. Dad had considerable experience working on the CB and Q in Nebraska, but California and the Santa Fe railroad operated with a whole different set of standards and rules. My dad would have to go to school for the Santa Fe Railroad while waiting to get hired on as an engineer.

During that time, my dad also had to provide for the family. Having grown up on a farm, he knew how to raise animals. So, he decided to try raising Pomeranian dogs. The business prospered, and the little dogs brought in a substantial amount of money for the family.

Eventually, my dad passed his railroad test for the Santa Fe

Railroad and was hired on as an engineer. In 1948, the Santa Fe asked my dad to be the engineer on the train that would transport Harry Truman, then President of the United States, from Los Angeles to San Diego.

Photo from Irwin Family Archives

John G. Irwin Sr. in his Santa Fe 2357 switch engine.

Dad ran the Presidential train all the way from L.A. to the beautiful Santa Fe Depot in downtown San Diego. His job was done. He wanted to get off the engine and avoid the huge crowd waiting to see the President.

Dad looked out one side of the engine and saw thousands of people waiting to hear the president speak. Then he looked out of the other side of the engine. No one was there. That's where he headed. Grabbing his grip, he got off the engine and started making his way to his car as fast as possible. Suddenly, he encountered a man walking along the deserted track.

It was President Harry Truman, who had somehow escaped his Secret Service detail for a moment of peace and quiet!

"I've been with those sons of bitches all day. You're the engineer, aren't you?" President Truman asked.

"I am," Dad said.

Photo from Irwin Family Archives

LaVon and John Irwin with baby Tommy in the middle.

Dad walked with the President for several minutes before the Secret Service caught up with them.

The President wished my dad well, then my dad stepped into his car and drove home (I would imagine at a higher than normal rate of speed) to tell my mother what had just happened. I can still remember dad reminiscing about that assignment.

The next big event in the life of the Irwin family happened in 1949. That's when my mom and dad had me, little Tommy Joe Irwin! I was kind of a late arrival. My brother, Greg, was 14 at the time and brother Bob was 10. They would both go on to attend Saint Augustine High School in East San Diego.

Greg was in drama class and one of his classmates was a heavy-set kid named Victor Buono. Greg and Victor were selected to act in a play at the Russ Auditorium. I remember, as a young kid, going to watch my brother Greg and Victor in the play, "The Barretts of Wimpole Street."

After high school, Victor Buono continued to pursue acting. Playing the Shakespearian character Falstaff at San Diego's famed Old Globe Theater, he was spotted by a talent agent … and it was off to Hollywood. He did small parts in movies and television shows – I remember seeing him on "Batman" and then "The Untouchables" – and then he hit a home run.

Appearing with screen legends Bette Davis and Joan Crawford in a movie called *What Ever Happened to Baby Jane?*, Buono garnered Academy and Golden Globe nominations for best supporting actor. He went on to have a long career as a character actor in movies and television until his death in 1982.

Greg, meanwhile, decided to join the Army and was stationed overseas in Germany. My other brother, Bob, was still in high school and became a great high school football player. After high school, Bob also joined the Army and headed off to Europe, in his case to Belgium.

As for me, I went to our Lady of the Sacred Heart Catholic School in East San Diego.

My dad had another brush with fame. San Diego's KOGO TV was developing an afternoon kids show, to be hosted by an actor costumed as a railroad engineer. My dad was involved in filming the show's opening. Dad had to pull the red 347C Santa Fe "Warbonnet" F7 engine into the depot, but he had to crouch down on his knees. All the audience would see through the cabin window would be the actor.

Dad had to stop the engine. Stepping down the ladder, the actor would walk into the depot. Cameras would then cut to the TV studio and the actor would walk through a studio mockup of the depot door saying, "Howdy, Howdy, Howdy, kids, good to see ya, good to see ya." The actor was Johnny Downs, who'd played Johnny in the *Our Gang* comedies, known as *The Little Rascals* in TV syndication. As an adult, Johnny Downs made it into the movies as a song-and-dance man. IMDb, the Internet Movie Database used by all of Hollywood to track movies, TV shows and creative careers, credits him with 105 movie/TV appearances.

I remember his show, sponsored by Golden Arrow Dairy. The producers would chroma key Johnny, dancing on top of the Golden Arrow dairy milk bottle with Bill Haley and the Comets singing, "Everybody Razzle Dazzle." At that time, I must have been six or seven years old. I regularly watched Johnny Downs on TV, as did thousands of other kids in San Diego. But I was the only one who knew who was really at the controls of the train bringing him into the station.

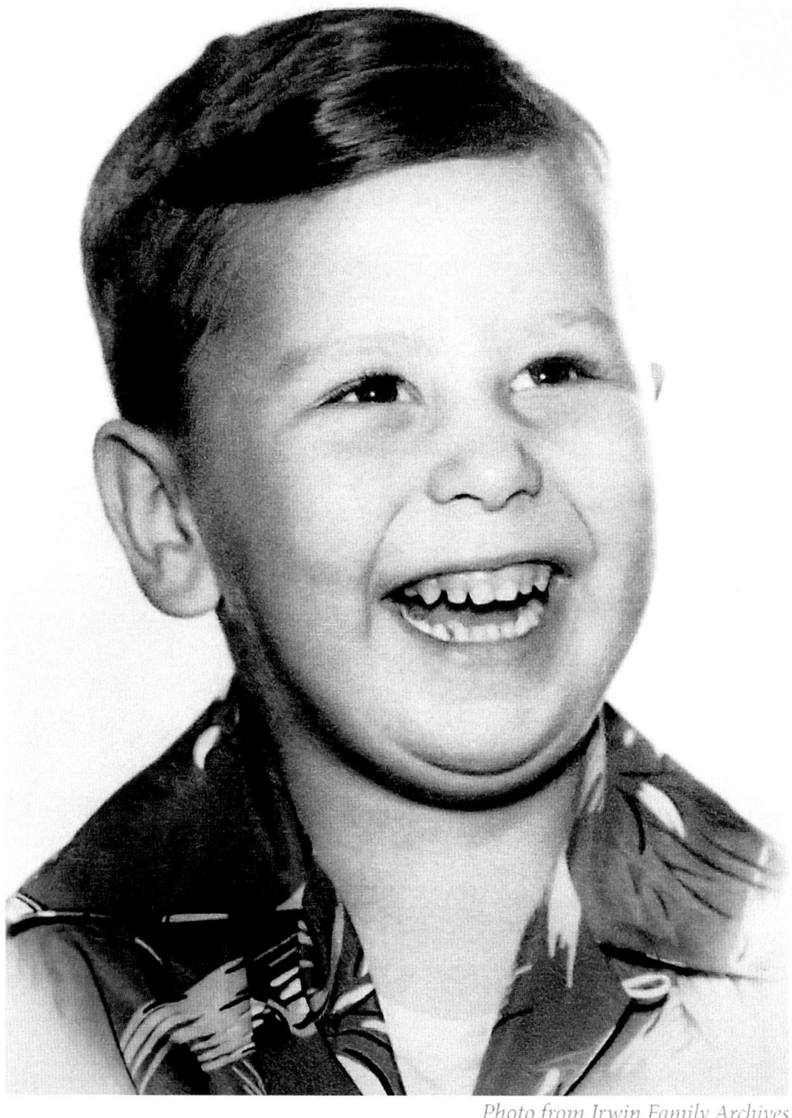

Photo from Irwin Family Archives

Tommy Irwin, age 6.

When I was 10, our family moved from East San Diego to a suburb called Lemon Grove, just east of the San Diego city limits. I switched schools and went to St. John of the Cross Catholic School in Lemon Grove.

Photo from Irwin Family Archives

An 8-year-old Tommy Irwin when he discovered the ranger hat.

My mom was a huge radio fan, and one day she was listening to DJ Frank Thompson, who was doing a remote broadcast from the KOGO Radio mobile studio in the parking lot of a Lemon Grove shopping center.

When I got home from school that day my mom said, "Tommy, there is a man on the radio broadcasting in Lemon

Grove and he's putting people on the air. Why don't you go down and see the man on the radio? Maybe he'll put you on the air."

Always the obedient son, I hopped on my bike and rode to see the man on the radio. I looked in the window of the trailer and saw Frank Thompson with two turntables and a microphone. I was fascinated. Thompson saw me looking through the window and said, "This is Frank Thompson on KOGO Radio and there's a young man looking through the window here in the KOGO Radio mobile studio. Come in here, young man. What is your name?" I told him my name and that I attended St. John of the Cross Catholic School in Lemon Grove.

Photo from Irwin Family Archives

Frank Thompson.

"Well, Tom," Frank said, "I've got four tickets for you to see the L.A. T-Birds roller derby team when they come to Westgate Park!"

I guess I was excited to get those tickets, but as I pedaled home, I kept thinking about that man in the mobile studio, the shiny, fascinating electronic gizmos he operated, and, most of all, that microphone, which could broadcast his voice all over the city.

I just kept thinking about it, and before too long I built my own little radio station in my bedroom.

Frank Thompson continued doing remote broadcasts around San Diego. That gave me the opportunity to see him whenever he was on location in the KOGO mobile studio. While I was at these events, I met another kid who was also a Frank Thompson follower. His name is Bill Martin.

Frank would take a break and let Bill start the record out of the NBC newscast. I said to myself, "Wow! I wish I could do that."

One day I got my chance. Bill hadn't arrived yet. Frank took a break and asked me to start the record. Bill showed up and found me sitting at the controls. He looked at the VU meter on the control board and said, "Hey, the needle is in the red, you've got to back off on the volume!"

I did what he said and gradually, over time, united by our shared passion for radio, we backed off our rivalry and became friends. To this day, Bill Martin remains one of my oldest and dearest friends.

End Run Around Phyllis

After seeing Frank Thompson in the KOGO Radio mobile studio and going home and building my own radio station in my bedroom, I wanted more. I wanted to see more radio studios. But who's going to let a 12-year-old into a professional radio studio?

The only one I knew who might help me was Frank Thompson. I asked Frank if I could come and see him at Broadcast City at the corner of 47th Street and Highway 94, home of KOGO TV and Radio, AM and FM.

Frank said it was OK, so I rode my bike to Broadcast City on a Saturday. I rode through Lemon Grove past College Grove, but there was one part of Highway 94 that I had to ride on to get to the 47th Street turn-off. That part of the freeway was off limits to pedestrian and bicycle traffic.

I took my chances. Lo and behold, a San Diego

police officer saw me on the freeway and stopped me. He said, "Son, it's not safe for you to be on this highway with your bike. Didn't you see the sign?"

"No, officer, I didn't. I'm sorry," I replied.

"I'm afraid I'm going to have to give you a ticket."

That was my first traffic violation. And it happened on my bike!

I finally reached Broadcast City and was able to get in to see Frank do his show in a professional studio rather than a remote studio. It was exciting, but KOGO was a "middle of the road" station. They played adult hits from performers like Sinatra, Ella Fitzgerald, and others. They were very gifted artists, but they just didn't fire my 12-year-old rocket.

I wanted to see the radio stations that played rock 'n' roll. In those days, those stations were KGB, KDEO and KCBQ.

KCBQ's studio was in downtown San Diego across from the El Cortez Hotel, which sits atop a hill and is famous for its glass elevator. Built in 1927, the hotel was the tallest building in San Diego for years.

Among the guests who stayed at the El Cortez were Elvis Presley, Bing Crosby, and Presidents Eisenhower, Johnson and Ford.

In the Seventies, the El Cortez would be home to some of the early San Diego Comic-Cons.

Right across the street from that iconic hotel, on the second floor at 7th and Ash, was the KCBQ studio, with its huge picture window looking out over the city. People could stand on the sidewalk and look up at the DJ doing his show. There was even a mirror on the ceiling so you could watch the DJ's hands cueing up the records and operating the control board.

Many young, future broadcasters would stand at that corner for hours watching KCBQ personalities Jerry Walker, Harry "Happy Hare" Martin, Don Howard, Scotty Day, Johnny Holliday, Shamus Patrick O'Hara and Shadow Jackson do their shows.

There was a PA speaker outside the window so you could hear the station as you stood in the street. I stood there many a time, dreaming of how someday I might get to broadcast a show up there in that studio, running that beautiful audio console with all its colorful knobs and lights.

I wanted to walk into that studio and stand there with the DJ so badly! I would take pictures with my Kodak Brownie camera from the street below, but the pictures never turned out right because of the glare of the glass. So I decided to go upstairs and ask the lady at the front desk.

I still remember her name. It was Phyllis. I said, "Ma'am, my name is Tom Irwin and I'm doing a report for school on vocations. If possible, I'd like to go into the studio and get a picture of the control room and the DJ on the air."

She promptly told me, "No, son, you can't! If you want a picture, you'll have to take it from the street. We don't allow visitors in the studio."

I went back downstairs and looked up at the studio. So near and yet so far. It was frustrating.

Then I saw a man walking up Ash Street who I recognized from the KCBQ survey sheet, which they gave out in record stores, featuring the top 40 songs and pictures of the DJs.

It was Scotty Day. I'd heard him on the air many times, but didn't know he was the station's program director.

I approached him, introduced myself, and told him about my school project.

Then I asked, "Is there any way I could go up and take a picture in the studio?"

He looked at me and smiled. "Follow me, son." We went up the stairs into the lobby and there was Phyllis, who'd just thrown me out.

Scotty said, "I'm taking this young man into the studio so he can get a better photo." Phyllis glared at me.

When we got into the studio, my Brownie camera was loaded with slide film and a flash cube on top, ready to go. The radio personality on the air was Bill Bishop.

His real name was Jerry Bishop, but since Jerry Walker was the morning man and KCBQ management didn't want two Jerrys on the station at the same time, Bishop had to change his first name. Their names continued to have interesting stories of their own.

Photo from LIFE Magazine

The KCBQ studios at 7th and Ash in downtown San Diego.

Jerry Bishop went on to have a long radio and voice-over career, ending up as the announcer on "Judge Judy." Meanwhile, Jerry Walker later worked for just shy of 30 years at KNX AM Newsradio in Los Angeles using his real name, Harry Birrell.

I stood in the studio with Scotty Day and Bill Bishop, ready to snap the picture. I stepped back, took a breath, said a prayer and clicked the shutter. I only had one chance.

Don't blow it, I thought, sweating bullets as I waited for the film to be developed and returned to me.

Then I got the picture. Thank goodness, everything turned out great. I still have it today. Blown up to 30x30, it hangs in my garage "pool hall," a regular Saturday night hangout for fellow DJs and friends to this day. That beautiful custom KCBQ audio console with Bill (Jerry) Bishop seated in front of it.

Some other young, aspiring disc jockeys who used to stand and look up at the KCBQ studios around that time include Neil Ross, Gene Knight, Brian White, Jim Duncan and Phil Flowers. Near the end of his long radio career, Phil Flowers returned to KCBQ, now a talk station under new ownership.

Phil did a show Sunday evenings that took its name from a bumper sticker the station had given out in its heyday that said: "I Q in my car!" Phil called his show, "I (still) Q in my car." He played airchecks of the station in its glory days from his extensive collection and became KCBQ's Official Historian.

Eventually, all of us young guns would get our chance to run the KCBQ audio console, but not in that window studio. By the time we got to KCBQ, the station had moved the whole operation east, to the San Diego suburb of Santee. The beautiful console was there, but it was in a plain, windowless room. (Well, there was a window, but it just gave you a view of an adjacent studio).

My longtime friends, DJs Don Howard and Gary Allyn, remembered broadcasting from the 7th and Ash studio. When I told them how much I'd wanted to work up there, they confessed it wasn't that great.

When the sun hit the glass, it sometimes became unbearably hot. And there wasn't any privacy. They said they sometimes felt like an exhibit in the zoo. But I still wish I could've been on the air there ... just once.

Photo from Irwin Family Archives

Bill Bishop on the air at the old KCBQ studios at 7th and Ash, in a photo taken by a 12-year-old Tommy Irwin!

First Radio Gigs

When I was 15, I started hanging out at KDEO Radio, a small 1,000-watt station licensed to the San Diego suburb of El Cajon. KDEO was a Top 40 radio station competing with the much higher-powered KCBQ and KGB.

The KDEO studios were a lot closer to where I lived, and it was a much more laid-back operation. There weren't any Phyllises around to keep me out.

The jocks on the air then were Fred Kiemel in the morning, program director Jim Price during midday hours, Ray Willes in the afternoons and Robin Scott at night. Overnights were handled by Lee Shoblom, and Richard Clark was the weekend DJ. Tom Shaefer was news director.

Not too long after I started hanging around KDEO, DJ Chuck Cooper came over from KGB, where I would pester him on the request line while I was washing the family's dinner dishes. I watched him wheel into the KDEO parking lot in his Cadillac. I went over and introduced myself. Chuck remembered me from the KGB request lines and we soon became friends.

He is a colorful guy, with a lot of stories. While Chuck was at KGB, the radio station brought the Beatles to San Diego. Les Turpin, KGB's program director, ordered all the jocks to be at the concert for the press conference with the Beatles.

While backstage at Balboa Stadium, Chuck was smoking a cigarette. John Lennon walked up to Chuck and asked if he could bum four cigarettes. Chuck obliged and Lennon gave Paul, George and Ringo each a cigarette and lit one himself. They smoked them during the press conference. I still have a picture of the Beatles smoking Chuck's cigarettes.

I would hang out at the KDEO studio at night and watch Chuck do his show, and he would let me use the KDEO production room to record my radio shows for my little bootleg bedroom station. Using my Sony tape recorder, I would play the tapes that I made at KDEO on speakers that sat on our patio. I knew how to do that because a neighbor had shown me. He was the father of my friend, Tom Brown, who lived across the street. Mr. Brown would soon regret sharing this skill with me.

Making use of a handy telephone pole, I managed run a wire from my house across the street to Tom Brown's bedroom window. I hooked my wire up to the speaker on Tom's bedside clock radio. Now I actually had a listener!

Next, I installed a switch on the radio. When it was flipped one way, the radio functioned normally. But when flipped in the other direction, the speaker would play whatever I fed it from across the street.

Since my amplifier was supplying the juice, the radio didn't need to be turned on. It could even be unplugged and still my station would play. This turned out to be a fatal flaw.

One night, while Tom was at summer camp, I decided to create an all-night show for my own amusement. Unfortunately, Tom had left the switch in the wrong direction. Suddenly my show was booming into the Brown house. "Ladies and gentlemen, you're listening to a million-dollar weekend all weekend long with Tom Irwin!!" This was followed by an ear-splitting rock song.

Awakened from a sound sleep, Tom's dad staggered groggily around the house, trying to find the source of the racket. Eventually he figured out what it was and began furiously turning the knobs on the radio, to no avail. Then he tried yanking the power plug out of the wall, but the cacophony continued. He picked up the radio, intending to hurl it at the wall, but luckily that broke the wire and blessed silence ensued.

Understandably, Tom and I got an earful. And I was back to zero listeners.

I began to wonder if there was a way I could actually go on the air with a transmitter. I met this guy named Owen (Wes) Western, who was really into electronics. I asked him if there was any way I could have a real transmitter to broadcast on the AM radio band? "Yes, I have one for sale," he said.

For $25, I bought my first transmitter, hooked it up to my

Sony tape recorder and, just like that, I was on the air on 840 AM! I would only go on at night because I didn't think the FCC would track me down outside of office hours. At least, that was my theory.

Our signal spread out and broadcast for a good 30 miles. I know because Owen Western and Richard Clark drove around to see how far the signal stretched. The guys had their own transmitters, and they would go on at different times.

My ideas didn't stop there. How about selling actual radio time on my illegal radio station to fund it?

I contacted Memo Diaz at Gordo's Mexican Restaurant in Lemon Grove. We struck a deal to trade out food for advertising on my station. During my broadcast hours, Memo Diaz played my station in his restaurant, and I ate delicious meals. A great idea, but a bit risky. I had a friend, Rick Mariotti, who lived up on a hill in Lemon Grove. Rick suggested I bring the transmitter "up to my house and we'll get out even further on the air," he said. I left the transmitter at his house. That was a big mistake.

One day, while sitting in study hall at Mount Miguel High School, I tuned my transistor radio to 840 AM and, to my surprise, I heard a Stevie Wonder song.

I said to myself, "Oh my God, somebody's on our frequency!" Then I heard my voice and knew Rick had the transmitter on in the daytime!

FCC field engineer Clarence C. Spellman soon tracked our transmitter down. He spoke to Rick's astonished parents.

"Your son has violated the Communications Act of 1934, which is punishable by five years in prison and a $10,000 fine."

Understandably, that didn't sit well with Rick's dad. He took a sledgehammer to the transmitter. That was the end of that.

The FCC took it to the next step, conducting a hearing. Fortunately, Rick and I were let off with a warning. The FCC folks suggested we get third-class FCC licenses and broadcast legally.

I immediately went down to the FCC office, took the test for the third-class license, and passed.

Now I was legal to work at a professional radio station – and I was soon going to get my chance!

One day, I was hanging out after school at KDEO, watching Ray Willis do his afternoon show. The program director, "Sunny" Jim Price, stuck his head in the control room and asked me to step out in the hallway. I thought I was in trouble and he was going to kick me out. But that wasn't the case.

Jim told me he was thinking about adding a record to the playlist, and he wanted a teenager's opinion of the music. He said many stations around the country did not want to add this record because it sounded like a folk group and wouldn't fit on a rock 'n' roll station.

Jim sat me down in his office and played me the record. Then he asked me what I thought of it. "Mr. Price, this record is really great! I like it!" I said, without any exaggeration. It was *really good.*

Based on the strength of my reaction, Jim decided to add the record to the playlist, making KDEO the first radio station in the country to play it. The song was the Mamas and the Papas' "California Dreamin'."

Soon other San Diego stations began playing it. Then powerhouse 93 KHJ in Los Angeles added it as well.

The song would go on to sell millions nationwide, certified Gold by the Recording Industry Association of America in 1966. It's such a great song, one of the signature tunes of the 1960s, and I'm glad I had a small part to play in its success.

Not too long after that, Jim Price asked me if I'd like to work for KDEO. He said the station needed someone to help out Chuck Cooper at his remote broadcasts from the car show at the San Diego Community Concourse, handing out swag to the listeners and ripping the news off the on-location teletype machine. The job paid $1.25 an hour. Was I interested? *Was I?!*

"Yes, of course!" I said.

Jim told me to talk to news director Tom Shaefer for instructions on how to work with the teletype machine. Tom and I eventually became good friends.

Now I had a gofer job at a real radio station, but still, I wanted be on the air. KDEO hired a guy named George Manning to do weekends. George's weekday job was program director of KPRI 106.5 FM in San Diego. While I was watching George do his KDEO weekend show he asked me if I'd be interested in doing Sunday mornings, 6 a.m. to noon, on KPRI FM.

Photo from Irwin Family Archives

A 16-year Tom Irwin, on the air at KPRI 106.5 FM.

Hard as it may be to believe today, FM radio didn't have many listeners back then. Inexpensive FM radios weren't being manufactured, and the home tuner, amplifier, and speaker combo you needed cost about as much as a top-of-the-line TV.

FM radios in cars were virtually nonexistent. I wouldn't have much of an audience. Also, the station played sappy middle-of-the-road music, which wasn't my cup of tea.

But it was an on-the-air job at a real radio station, and I was sure to have more listeners than I did on my bootleg bedroom station. I started the following Sunday morning. It was 1966. I was 16 years old, and my radio journey had begun!!

Junior Achievement

Before we get further into my career story, I want to double back and pay tribute to a wonderful organization that was so helpful to me in my youth.

When I was a freshman at Mount Miguel High School in 1965, I went to the vocational counselor's office and found out that there was an organization called Junior Achievement. It allowed high school kids, with adult supervision, to start an actual company, produce and sell an actual product, and run their company.

I immediately zeroed in on Junior Achievement broadcasting. The group met once a week at KOGO Radio and produced weekly radio shows. The shows were called "Teen Scene" and "Youth on the Go." Both shows aired on KOGO.

We played the standard middle-of-the road music that KOGO featured – Tony Bennett, Frank Sinatra – plus songs by younger artists such as Petula Clark, The Seekers and even Simon and Garfunkel.

However, we weren't allowed to play rock 'n' roll. There were several jobs available to students. Some of the kids didn't want to be on the radio. They wanted to sell radio time. Other kids, like Chuck Branch, wanted to run the equipment and produce the shows.

Then there were people like me, John Bolin, Bruce Oldham, Fred Ashman and Larry DeRusha, who wanted to be on the air.

The sales part of our little company was supervised by our sales advisor from KOGO Radio, Mike Tully. The programming side fell under the direction of Dick Roberts, the program director of KOGO Radio.

I often wondered why Mike Tully and Dick Roberts, who worked all day at the radio station, would come back at night and help us kids produce a radio show.

Years later, I asked Dick Roberts that question, and he told me that when he was 16 and in high school, he started the very first Junior Achievement broadcasting company. It was in New Bedford, Massachusetts, on WNBH Radio. The program had given him his start and he'd decided to pay it back by paying it forward.

Mike Tully told all of us who wanted to be on the air that the time would come when we'd have to eventually move into sales or management because of age. "You can't be 'Big Daddy' on the air forever," he said.

He told us that once a radio disc jockey turns 35, he or she should think about moving elsewhere in the radio station organization. Or some other business entirely. Imagine, 35 was considered too old to be a DJ!

Yet, there's some truth in that. Most DJs don't get to develop or enjoy the long on-air careers that I and a relative handful of others have experienced. For every happy ending like mine, there are hundreds of unhappy tales about jocks who didn't take the off-ramp in time.

Our Junior Achievement broadcasters went on to have great careers in radio and television. John Bolin got his degree in radio and television at San Diego State and worked at several radio stations such as KLRO Stereo 95, KFMX FM and KSON AM. Today, John is a successful representative for Sony Television.

Bruce Oldham got into television at KTLA Los Angeles and ran camera on many television shows, including "The Tonight Show" with Conan O'Brien. Another broadcaster, Larry DeRusha, went on to work at KFMB TV on the "Regis Philbin Show" and eventually ended up working in Hollywood for Norman Lear on shows like "All in the Family," "The Jeffersons" and "Maude."

In addition, Fred Ashman became a television director and eventually started his own company called Multi Image, which created shows for many conventions that came to San Diego. Multi Image has made millions of dollars. And Chuck Branch, who was one of the kids who wanted to run the equipment to produce the shows, became a recording studio engineer and has designed many top-notch recording studios. All of us owe much to Junior Achievement for helping us start.

Junior Achievement continues to help countless high school kids get into business and be successful.

Photo from Irwin Family Archives

Row one, from left: Eric Kehew, Steve Tivel, Danny Alvarez, Dick Roberts (advisor), Mike Tully (advisor), Charles Branch. Row two, from left: Unidentified, Bruce Tokars, Bob Peral, Larry DeRusha, Carleton Seely, John Bolin, Tom Irwin, Judy Swim, Mike Pulli, Tony Pulli.

Getting My "Ticket"

When I graduated from Mount Miguel High School in 1968, I was no longer working at KPRI FM, and it was time to get that first-class FCC license.

In the studio of every AM radio station that I visited, I saw framed blue certificates on the wall – first-class licenses. AM radio was king in those days, and many of those stations needed DJs who held these licenses.

It's a bit complicated but basically, AM stations that operated above a certain power or used a directional signal required a first-class operator on duty at all times.

In the old days, there were transmitter engineers and announcers, but station owners figured out that if they could hire DJs with those licenses, the jocks could spin the records and monitor the transmitter at the same time. One person doing two jobs. A big money saver.

Chuck Cooper told me that if I ever hoped to have a meaningful radio career, I needed to get the license. Guys in the business called them "tickets" because they were in such demand that they were effectively a "ticket" to employment.

I asked Chuck if he knew of any schools that could help me get the license. Without hesitation, he recommended the William B. Ogden Radio Operational Engineering School in Burbank.

A lot of famous guys went to Ogden's to get their first-class licenses, including Neil Ross and Jhani Kaye. And when my good friend Jack Vincent was going to the Don Martin School of Radio and Television in Hollywood in the Fifties, that's where Bill Ogden taught the first-class license course before opening his own school in Burbank.

I found it amazing how many people I met later in my broadcasting career previously attended the Ogden school. Years after I got my license, my friend Gary Kelley and I were in the audience for George Putnam's "Talk Back to the News" show on KTLA Channel 5 in Los Angeles. George did a newscast in front of a studio audience, followed by a segment in which audience members could come up to a microphone and talk about the news or just about anything else.

I don't know exactly why I did it, but suddenly I found myself walking up to that mic. I said, "My name is Shotgun Tom Kelly and I would like to salute one great man, Bill Ogden." I started to talk about Bill and his school and how he had helped so many people get a start in broadcasting.

George interrupted me. "There must be a lot of truth in what you're saying, Tom. I just noticed every cameraman in the studio is raising his hand. Are you guys all former students?" The cameramen, hands held high, nodded enthusiastically. I'll never forget that moment, and I found out later that Bill was actually watching the telecast!

Two of my dear friends, Johnny Yount, who became Spanky Elliot at KACY, and Big John Carter at KYNO in Fresno, had already gone to the Ogden school and gotten their licenses. With those guys as my inspiration, I decided to give it a shot.

My friend Bob Neutzling, with whom I worked at KPRI, and our friend Norbert Gomes (who later became Jimi Fox and put KTNQ on the air in Los Angeles) all decided to enroll together. We paid our $450 tuition fee and soon were on our way to the school, now located in Huntington Beach, California.

At Ogden's, classes were held seven days a week, so we had to live in a dormitory at the school on Warner Avenue, just a few blocks from the beach. It was kind of a family operation. There was Bill Ogden, of course; his wife Tally; the secretary; and Tally's sister, Thora, who took care of coffee and tea breaks.

I remember Bill Ogden yelling: "Coffees! Get 'em high!!" This meant you were supposed to raise your hand and he would take a count on who wanted coffee and who wanted tea so Thora could fix it.

Bill Ogden was quite a character, probably the best teacher I have ever had. He specialized in getting this complicated electronic knowledge into our heads so we could pass the test.

Back then it seemed like almost everybody smoked, and we

were all welcome to smoke at Ogden's. There were ashtrays on our desks. Ogden smoked Salem cigarettes, and each time he lit up a cigarette, he'd put a Parke-Davis throat drop in his mouth. Then, sucking on the lozenge, Bill would lecture, pacing in front of the blackboard while smoking that Salem cigarette.

I recall one time prior to a class, I wrote on the blackboard, "All I want to do is play the hits" in capital letters. When Ogden came into the classroom and spotted my message, he asked who wrote it. I raised my hand and Ogden, in his irascible style, responded, "You're not playing ANYTHING until you learn this stuff."

Photo by Pat Maestro

Tom Irwin at the William B. Ogden
Radio Operational Engineering School.

Photo by Pat Maestro

Tom Irwin studying for his first-class FCC license.

His words rang true. The test had nothing to do with announcing or DJ work. Rather, we needed to know the rules and regulations of the FCC, along with plenty of electronics and mathematics.

Different types of entertainment or communications industry professionals attended Ogden's for all kinds of reasons. If you worked for the telephone company or operated radar equipment, you needed an FCC first-class license. If you worked for a television station, you also needed the license to run the television transmitter or a TV studio camera. I just wanted the license to get a job at a rock 'n' roll radio station and play the hits.

I met a lot of great guys while going to Ogden's. Some I remember are John Chappell and his friends Wes Page and Rick Myers. They all came from Modesto and wanted to head back home and work for KFIV (K5) in Modesto. It was an AM station broadcasting a directional signal and you needed that first-class license to work there.

Another great friend I met at Ogden's was "Your Duke" Dave Sholin. After he received his first-class license, he went to San Jose to work for KLIV. Dave later worked at "THE BIG 610" KFRC in San Francisco and then became co-owner of the Gavin Report, a highly respected periodical in the music and radio industry. Currently, Dave is involved in music promotion and does afternoons at KSJJ in Bend, Oregon.

Dave had a profound experience I'd like to share. When he was employed as the music director for RKO Radio, he was afforded the opportunity, through famed music industry executive David Geffen, to conduct an exclusive interview with John Lennon and Yoko Ono in New York for a network special. After the interview, John and Yoko were waiting outside their apartment for their car. Since it had not yet arrived, John asked Dave for a ride to the recording studio in his car. Once he and his driver dropped off John and Yoko, Dave continued to the airport to catch his flight back to San Francisco.

When his flight landed in San Francisco, Dave fetched his car from the airport parking lot. On his drive home, he tuned into his old station, KFRC. Bill Lee was on the air playing continuous Beatles songs. This wasn't normal for a rigidly formatted station like the big 610. *What was going on?* Dave thought to himself. Then Bill came on the air and announced that John Lennon had been shot and killed outside his New York apartment, the Dakota. While trapped aboard an airplane for the previous five-plus hours, Dave hadn't heard the news. He drove down the Bayshore Freeway, numb from the horror. John Lennon, the most famous of the Beatles, a man he'd seen only a few hours ago feeling so vibrant and alive, buoyed by the success of his first album in years, was dead. It didn't seem possible.

At midnight, Gary Cagle, KFRC's program director, called Dave and asked him to come down to the station. A few hours later, Dave was scheduled to appear on "Good Morning America." Dave's interview was the final interview John Lennon ever gave.

There are so many other guys I met at Ogden's who remain friends to this day like Bob Lang (The Du-Lang), Derek Waring and Frank Azevedo. Another good friend I met at Ogden's was Dirk Raaphorst, who eventually became Dirk Donovan at the "Big 13" KYNO in Fresno.

We all had dreams of one day working for Boss Radio 93 KHJ in Los Angeles, one of the most famous and successful Top 40 radio stations in the country. Top 40 radio was a true pop cultural phenomenon and helped usher in the rise of rock 'n' roll on radio in the Sixties.

As the name implies, Top 40 radio stations played the 40 or so most popular hits of the week, based on a formula that included requests, record sales and, quite often, the program director's whims.

The format was also known for its animated, wise-cracking DJs, with icons such as Cousin Brucie, Wolfman Jack and The Real Don Steele becoming welcome visitors in teen homes throughout the country, so close with listeners they might as well be family members.

The Top 40 format was introduced after the seven-inch 45 rpm "single" replaced the old 10-inch 78s, the vinyl record now smaller, lighter and less breakable. Top 40 radio also birthed the practice of weekly survey sheets listing the most popular songs, and even led to syndicated radio shows such as "American Top 40" that consisted of a countdown of the 40 most popular songs as ranked by *Billboard* or other trades, of which there were only a handful.

A radio consultant named Bill Drake refined the Top 40 format, cutting the playlist down to 30 songs, and brought it to stations around the country under the Boss Radio name. Boss Radio 93 KHJ was the mothership.

All of us young, aspiring DJs wanted to be as good as KHJ's two biggest DJ stars, Robert W. Morgan and The Real Don Steele. I didn't know it then, but in 1997, after The Real Don Steele passed away, program director Mike Phillips would ask me to come up to Los Angeles and succeed my radio hero at KRTH 101. More about that later.

I knew that before any visions of glory could even hope to materialize for me, I had to secure my first-class FCC license, pay my dues in smaller markets and work my way up. All of us studied hard at Ogden's to get that ticket. I remember studying late into the night while listening to all-night DJ Johnny Williams on 93 KHJ.

One song he used to play was "Gotta Get a Message to You" by the Bee Gees. Every time I hear that song today, I think of the hard sleepless nights we spent working and studying, sometimes with funny phrases of Bill Ogden's pouring through our heads, like "Voltage goes nowhere." Or, "That's not a head on your shoulders, that's a pimple that hasn't come to a head yet!"

A lot of guys complained when he would take a break from teaching and start talking about his life overseas as an Army instructor in mathematics and the places that he had visited. I think Ogden did that on purpose to give us a break in class when he sensed we were getting burned out.

As the days and the weeks went on, a lot of us prepared to go down to the FCC office and take the test for the second-class license and then the first-class license, elements one and three. Before they went down to take the test, my friends received the famous golden pencil that Ogden would give you when he decided you were ready.

He would say this pencil had magical qualities. If it saw you trying to write down the wrong answer, it would scream at you. The funny thing was, for some reason, the folks at the FCC couldn't seem to hear it.

We were punchy enough from lack of sleep by then to actually believe it. Some of the guys came back from the test swearing the pencil actually did scream at them a time or two.

As for me, I was having a real hard time trying to take in all that information. In truth, I almost gave up.

Then, one afternoon, a very famous announcer, Larry Huffman from KWIZ in Santa Ana, dropped by the school. I was sitting in the lobby, and I knew who Larry was because he did the voicing for the drag racing commercials on all the stations. Larry was production director at KWIZ and announcer at the Orange County International Raceway, the Lyons Dragstrip, and all sorts of other famous tracks.

He was known as the fastest mouth in the West. The *Los Angeles Times* nicknamed him "Supermouth."

I knew one other thing about Larry. He was a successful graduate of the Ogden school. I was quite depressed because all my friends had taken the test, passed and headed into their careers, and I was the only one left. Larry is an incredibly dynamic and positive guy. He gave me a pep talk that day as only he can. He said: "You can do this, Tom! I did it and I know you can too! Just don't give up!" If Larry hadn't given me that pep talk, I might have dropped out. I'll always be grateful for that wonderful boost he gave me.

It was getting close to December. Ogden came up to me and said, "OK, Tom, why don't you go try to pass that test? You know the information; you can do it." But Bill did not give me a gold pencil. I don't know if that was the reason or not, but I went down to the FCC office, sat down with a plain old #2 pencil – ya know, the non-magical kind - and started to work on the test. Sadly, I didn't pass.

After the holidays, I returned, rested and more determined than ever, and studied with a different class of guys for about four more weeks. Then Ogden called me in with a couple other guys and this time he gave us all the famous gold pencil

– even me. This time, I went down to the FCC office and took the test for the second time, much more confidently.

A week later, one of those blue pieces of paper for which I worked so hard arrived in the mail. It said: "First Class License – Thomas Joseph Irwin." I framed it, along with the gold pencil Ogden had given me. It now hangs in my "I Love Me" room.

Now, I was ready to get my radio career rolling.

A quick aside: Years later, the FCC made regulation changes. The first-class license was no longer needed. It was replaced by a yellow certificate called a general license. After all that

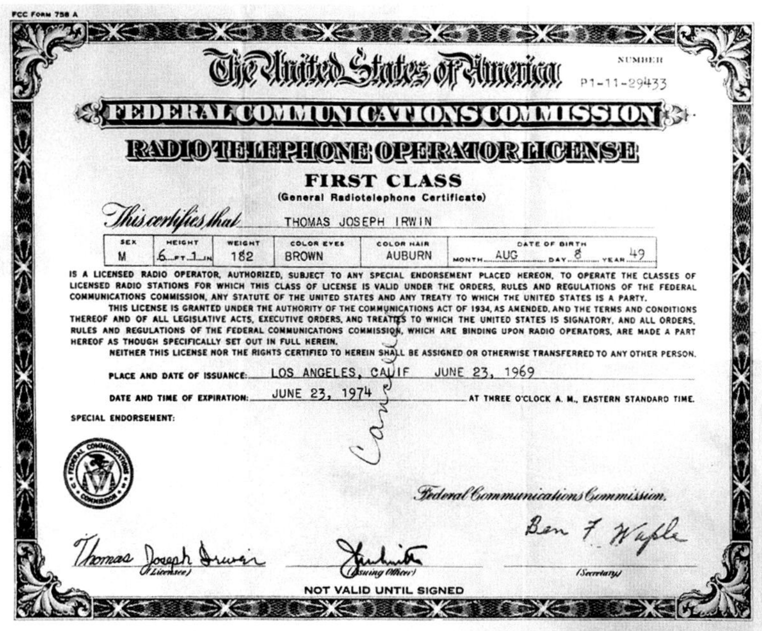

FCC FORM 758 A

The United States of America

NUMBER P1-11-29433

FEDERAL COMMUNICATIONS COMMISSION

RADIO TELEPHONE OPERATOR LICENSE

FIRST CLASS

(General Radiotelephone Certificate)

This certifies that THOMAS JOSEPH IRWIN

SEX	HEIGHT	WEIGHT	COLOR EYES	COLOR HAIR	DATE OF BIRTH
M	6 FT 1 IN	182	BROWN	AUBURN	MONTH AUG DAY 8 YEAR 49

IS A LICENSED RADIO OPERATOR, AUTHORIZED, SUBJECT TO ANY SPECIAL ENDORSEMENT PLACED HEREON, TO OPERATE THE CLASSES OF LICENSED RADIO STATIONS FOR WHICH THIS CLASS OF LICENSE IS VALID UNDER THE ORDERS, RULES AND REGULATIONS OF THE FEDERAL COMMUNICATIONS COMMISSION, ANY STATUTE OF THE UNITED STATES AND ANY TREATY TO WHICH THE UNITED STATES IS A PARTY.

THIS LICENSE IS GRANTED UNDER THE AUTHORITY OF THE COMMUNICATIONS ACT OF 1934, AS AMENDED, AND THE TERMS AND CONDITIONS THEREOF AND OF ALL LEGISLATIVE ACTS, EXECUTIVE ORDERS, AND TREATIES TO WHICH THE UNITED STATES IS SIGNATORY, AND ALL ORDERS, RULES AND REGULATIONS OF THE FEDERAL COMMUNICATIONS COMMISSION, WHICH ARE BINDING UPON RADIO OPERATORS, ARE MADE A PART HEREOF AS THOUGH SPECIFICALLY SET OUT IN FULL HEREIN.

NEITHER THIS LICENSE NOR THE RIGHTS CERTIFIED TO HEREIN SHALL BE ASSIGNED OR OTHERWISE TRANSFERRED TO ANY OTHER PERSON.

PLACE AND DATE OF ISSUANCE: LOS ANGELES, CALIF JUNE 23, 1969

DATE AND TIME OF EXPIRATION: JUNE 23, 1974 AT THREE O'CLOCK A. M., EASTERN STANDARD TIME.

SPECIAL ENDORSEMENT:

Federal Communications Commission.

Ben F. Waple (Secretary)

Thomas Joseph Irwin (Licensee)

(Issuing Officer)

NOT VALID UNTIL SIGNED

Photo from Irwin Family Archives

The coveted first-class FCC, awarded to one "Thomas Joseph Irwin".

work, my first-class license is no longer valid. I now have a general license. It hangs on my wall along with my expired blue "ticket."

Attending the class at Ogden's proved to be a great opportunity. It taught me how to study and take multiple-choice tests and pass. Bill Ogden would tell us, "Don't look at their answers; get the right answer in your head and then find it in the multiple choices. That'll be the right answer." To this day, I take my multiple-choice tests at the DMV the Bill Ogden way. But more important was the other lesson I learned: the value of perseverance.

I would need to use a lot of that in the coming years.

Merced, Ventura and Bakersfield

CHAPTER 8

Now that I had my first-class FCC license, it was time for me to go to work!

A lot of radio people live like nomads, traveling from city to city and state to state while racking up an increasing number of station call letters on their resumes. There are examples of DJs who manage to spend their entire careers in one city, but it's rare.

Other than a one-year stint in Phoenix, Arizona, I managed to spend my entire career working in one state, California. Most of my airtime was spent in two of Southern California's biggest cities, San Diego and Los Angeles.

Truth is, in the beginning, I would have lived just about anywhere to be on the radio.

Jim Price at Radio KDEO had told me that once I had my ticket, he'd put me on weekends. But I was strongly advised not to do that. If you come in as the weekend kid, they always think of you as the weekend kid. You'll find yourself being passed over for the prime air shifts in favor of some guy from out of town.

My old friend Bob Neutzling had moved to Merced, California, where he took on the job of program director at KYOS. Bob offered me the night show, from seven to midnight. I took it.

I remember the No. 1 song in 1969 was Bob Dylan's "Lay Lady Lay." Every time I hear it, it takes me back to the beginning of my career.

It was so much fun being on an AM station playing rock 'n' roll, and KYOS had a picture window studio. As you know, I always dreamed of working in a studio where people from the outside could look in at you doing a show, like KCBQ at 7th and Ash in San Diego.

I had so much fun in Merced, but it was a small town and I wanted to see if I could make it bigger. So, after I'd been at KYOS for six months, I sent a tape to KACY in Port Hueneme, California, a small coastal town in Ventura County, just north of Los Angeles, and they hired me. I heard that early on in their careers, legendary L.A. DJs Robert W. Morgan and Bob Eubanks had worked there and it was a steppingstone to Los Angeles. In Bob's case, it led to hosting one of the most popular television shows of the late Sixties and early Seventies, "The Newlywed Game". I was in the lobby at KACY and the program director, Bill Tanner, walked in and said, "Hi, Bobby!"

"Are you talking to me?" I asked.

"Yes, if you are going to work here your name is going to be Bobby McAllister."

I wasn't sure about that. I wanted to use my real name, Tom Irwin, like I did at KYOS. But it looked like that wasn't going to happen.

They started "Bobby McAllister" out on the all-night show. KACY, "Boss of the Beach," operated at 10,000 watts in the daylight hours and 1,000 watts at night. After a while, they promoted me to the 6 p.m.- to-midnight show. My family and friends could hear me in San Diego just before the power change at sunset.

Photo from Irwin Family Archives

The newly renamed Bobby McAllister.

As I was driving into work one afternoon, I heard the disc jockey who preceded me on the air, Dave Conley, say "Bobby 'Shotgun' McAllister is coming up at 6 p.m.!" I liked that name, especially the middle name, so I became Bobby "Shotgun" McAllister.

Dave Conley and I grew very close. When he finally got the program director job at KAFY in Bakersfield, his dream job, he invited me to come along with him and said I could use my real name, Tom Irwin.

Off Dave and I went to Bakersfield. KAFY was more like L.A. and San Francisco's Boss Radio stations KHJ and KFRC. KAFY's jingles were even sung by the same group that did jingles for those stations – the Johnny Mann Singers.

When we arrived in Bakersfield and met the general manager, everything went well but, unfortunately, it looked like I wouldn't be able to use Tom Irwin after all.

The GM said, "You know, I like the name Tom, but Irwin doesn't flow well, especially in a jingle." Then he began pairing "Tom" with several different two-syllable last names, like Tom Connor, Tom Stewart, and, finally, Tom Kelly.

When he said "Tom Kelly" he stopped and repeated the two names a couple of times, smiled and said, "OK, how about Tom Kelly?" Dave Conley jumped in, smiling and animated. "Great! We can revive the Shotgun from Bobby 'Shotgun' McAllister and you'll be Shotgun Tom Kelly."

I instantly fell in love with the name, and I've used it ever since.

Not long after I went on the air at KAFY, playing the hits as Shotgun Tom Kelly, I picked up a side hustle. Cliff Cox, the program director of KERO Television Channel 23, said they were looking for somebody to play a character named Nemo the Clown in a Saturday morning children's show. Was I interested?

This fell right into another of my broadcasting dreams: to do a children's show like the one I used to watch in San Diego with Johnny Downs when I was a kid. I jumped at the chance.

Every Saturday morning, I would put on all of that make-up and transform into Nemo the Clown. After the show, still

Photo from Irwin Family Archives

Nemo!

Photo from Irwin Family Archives

Nemo the Clown in action.

dressed as Nemo, I would make personal appearances at the independent grocers of Bakersfield.

I used to interview kids on the show. One time, a kid came out of the peanut gallery and asked me a question and I couldn't come up with an answer.

I can't remember what the question was, but I do remember the kid saying, "Nemo, don't you know the answer to that question?"

I replied, "Of course I do - Nemo ain't *stupid*!"

Future movie and television writer Ken Levine was working at KERN Radio in Bakersfield and watching that Saturday morning when I said, "Nemo ain't stupid."

To this day, he thinks that's one of the funniest lines he's ever heard.

After being at KAFY for nearly two years, from 1968 to 1970, I heard there was an opening at KGB Boss Radio 136 in my hometown, San Diego. I sent a tape of my KAFY show to program director Charlie Van Dyke.

Shortly thereafter, I got a phone call from Charlie. "Shotgun, I got your tape and it sounds too good to be true!" Charlie said. "In the next couple of weeks, when you least expect it, I'm coming to Bakersfield to listen to you live, so do some good shows!"

One night from the control room, about two weeks later, I looked out the window and who do I see but Charlie Van

Dyke, listening to my show. When I was finished, he came into the radio station and said, "Let's go out to dinner."

Afterward, he asked, "Shotgun, how bad do you want to work at KGB?"

"Charlie, more than anything in this world," I said, and I meant every word.

He extended his hand. "Welcome to KGB."

My first day at KGB, Charlie handed me business cards and notepads with my name on them. Then he said, "Shotgun, tomorrow report to Cinara photography studio and get your picture taken for the Boss 30."

This was the survey of the top 30 records which was printed up and handed out at record stores all over San Diego. It had been my dream to one day get my picture on The KGB Boss 30 survey ... and now that dream was coming true!

From KGB To KCBQ

What an amazing moment, working at a great radio station back in my hometown. It had all happened so fast it seemed too good to be true!

Unfortunately, it was. After I spent about six months at KGB, big changes happened at cross-town rival KCBQ. The station brought in a new program director, Buzz Bennett, along with his assistant, Rich "Brother" Robbin. Buzz proceeded to fire most of the KCBQ DJs and replace them with his guys.

One of the jocks he fired was the legendary K.O. Bayley. K.O. had worked for Bill Drake, the originator of the Boss Radio format, which we utilized at KGB.

Drake had originated the format in Fresno, then taken control of KGB in San Diego and eventually stations all over the country. K.O. had been part of Drake's original lineup at KYNO in Fresno and had worked at other Drake stations including KGB in San Diego, KFRC in San Francisco and WOR FM in New York. When Buzz fired him at KCBQ, the first thing K.O. did was call Bill Drake. Drake wanted K.O. back in the fold and decided to put him on KGB. But to make room for K.O., somebody needed to go.

Guess who?

Officially I was told that I was too "green" to work at KGB. I would be transferred to their Fresno station and maybe moved up later, when I was ready.

With all due respect to the fine folks in Fresno, this was the last thing I wanted. San Diego was my hometown and I wanted to stay. Plus, Fresno was a much smaller market. It was a big step down, kind of like a Major League Baseball player being sent back to the farm team. Charlie Van Dyke told me the switch would happen in two weeks. What was I going to do?

I called my old friend Linda. A few years later we would marry, but at the time we were just good friends. Linda was working in the traffic department at KCBQ, scheduling programs and commercials. I was just looking for a shoulder to cry on, but Linda proceeded to do me a huge life-changing solid.

As luck would have it, one of the KCBQ DJs had just given notice. They needed a replacement, pronto. Linda marched into Buzz Bennett's office and put in a pitch for me. She told Buzz and Rich that I would be the perfect guy.

She did such a good job of selling them on me that they agreed to listen to my show on KGB that night.

Lucky for me, they liked what they heard, and they made me an offer which I happily accepted. Now instead of flying off to Fresno, all I had to do was drive out to the KCBQ studios in scenic Santee.

When I walked into Buzz Bennett's office, he announced that he was going to give me a two-week paid vacation. But he had an assignment he wanted me to complete during that time: to read a book titled *The Power of Your Subconscious Mind* by Joseph Murphy.

"You see," said Buzz, "all of us here at KCBQ operate on positive vibrations. There are no negatives in this radio station."

Truthfully, I'm not much of a reader, but I did manage to read the book in case Buzz decided to hit me with a pop quiz. I'm sure I didn't get all of it, but basically the book says that you can use your imagination to suggest ideas to your subconscious to get what you want. Then, your subconscious mind will point you toward making those ideas a reality, without you even realizing it.

This all sounded pretty "woo woo" to me. But I did read the book and liked what it had to say. I've always been a pretty positive guy anyway.

When I finally broadcast my first show on KCBQ, a happy surprise awaited me. The station had closed its glassed-in studio in downtown San Diego and moved the entire operation to the transmitter in Santee. My dream to one day broadcast from that downtown studio would never happen, but it turned out all the equipment had made the journey!

I finally got my hands on that beautiful custom-made audio console on which I had watched so many of my favorite radio personalities like Don Howard, Johnny Holiday, Scotty Day, Seamus Patrick O'Hara and Shadow Jackson operate. I was really excited!

Listen to Shotgun Tom's aircheck at KCBQ.

AM To FM Phoenix To San Diego

KCBQ and Boss Radio KGB were in a battle for the ratings. When ratings battles take place, anything goes when it comes to promotions. Each station was trying to outdo the other with contests and stunts.

Singer Janis Joplin was riding high on an unlikely hit at the time called "Mercedes Benz." She sang it acapella with just the sound of her foot tapping time. It contained the line, "Oh Lord, won't you buy me a Mercedes Benz?"

Feeding off the popularity of the song, KCBQ announced a contest. The grand prize would be a classic Mercedes Benz.

Not to be outdone, across town, Charlie Van Dyke announced a promotion, declaring: "Boss Radio 136 KGB is giving away the home of your dreams!!"

The station bought a new tract home and gave it

away on the air! It didn't help: KCBQ just kept rocketing up in the ratings with KGB a distant second.

Our slogan at the time was "KCBQ keeps on truckin'!" And that's just what we did. We only used one jingle before every record. It was part of a jingle package produced by the previous KCBQ program director, Gary Allyn.

There were about 30 different jingles in the package, but Buzz used only one. It started with a fast drum roll followed by the call letters sung fast and loud. It sounded like a rocket ship taking off. Buzz called it the shotgun jingle, though there was no reference to me.

Photo from Irwin Family Archives

Shotgun Tom, on the air at KCBQ.

I had my own shotgun jingle. It started with the singers singing "Shotgun Tom!" followed by a shotgun blast sound effect and the singers jumping back in for "KCBQ!"

Buzz Bennett operated a lot on instinct, which led to some surprising outcomes at times. One involved Rod Stewart, who had recently left the Jeff Beck Group to become a solo artist.

I walked into Buzz's office one day. The record promoter from Mercury Records was visiting the station, and he had a brand-new single by Rod, "Reason to Believe," a folksy tune written, composed and first recorded by Tim Hardin in 1965. The record guy said, "This is gonna be a big hit and we want KCBQ to be the first station to play it."

Buzz took a listen to the song. "That's really nice." Then he asked the record promoter to play the flip side.

The record promoter said, "No, no, no, no! That's a terrible song. Rod Stewart doesn't even like it. It was just a song to fill the 'B' side."

Buzz insisted on hearing it anyway. When he did, he fell in love with it. The song? "Maggie May". Buzz not only added the song to the KCBQ playlist, but he also created a contest, asking the listeners to count the number of times we played the song.

Buzz made it so easy for everyone to get the correct number of times we played "Maggie May" that everybody who entered the contest had the right answer. They could enter as many times as they wanted. We filled a big dump truck in the parking lot of the station with entries. The ultimate winner sent in 500 entries. He won a thousand dollars.

Rod Stewart did even better. KCBQ made so much noise with our contest that other stations took note and began playing the 'B' side of Rod's new record, too. "Maggie May" established Stewart as a solo artist and became one of his biggest hits in a 50-year career filled with them.

Another record that Buzz promoted in 1971 was the brand-new John Lennon single "Imagine." Buzz made a deal with Apple Records. We would give the song tons of promotion if KCBQ could be the first station in the world to play it. The newest single by a Beatle, put out just a year after the band broke up. For about a month, we promoted that KCBQ would have the world exclusive of the much-anticipated new John Lennon song.

When the time came, we arranged for the acetate disc to be flown down from Los Angeles on PSA Airlines. The station arranged for a motorcycle escort and an armored truck to transport the record out to KCBQ in Santee. We had television coverage on the road and in the studio. Buzz said we'd premiere the record on my show.

The song arrived at the station. Rich "Brother" Robbin was assigned the task of copying the disc to a tape cartridge in the production studio. He wrote the title of the song on the cartridge label and gave it to my intern, who brought it to me in the studio. There was a bank of television news cameras pointed at me. I was a little nervous, to put it mildly.

I keyed the mic, took a quick peek at what Rich had scribbled on the tape cartridge label and said, "Ladies and gentlemen, you've been waiting all month for KCBQ to play the brand-new John Lennon song. Well, it's finally here and right now on the Shotgun Tom Kelly show here is the world premiere of John Lennon's new song … 'IMOGENE!!'"

Just as I finished the intro, Linda came into the control room, after holding a very furious Rich back by his shirt. I stood up with a huge grin on my face and said, "Well, how did I do?"

"Um, well, not too good. Rich is outside the control room ready to strangle you," Linda said. She wasn't smiling.

I was in total shock. I even hit the vocal without previewing the record, so I thought I did great. Linda burst my bubble when she told me that the name of the song was "Imagine," NOT "Imogene."

I was horrified. I remember after the record ended going back on the air and saying something like: "Hey, folks, you know I was just messing with you. The song's title is obviously 'Imagine.'"

In my defense, the combination of my nervousness and Rich's poor penmanship had led to an enormous gaffe. Rich had written with a black sharpie pen on the cartridge "IM A GINE." I quickly looked at the title and pronounced the word, or so I thought, phonetically. I can visualize it to this day and still cringe when I think about it.

Another inventive idea of Buzz Bennett's was to dupe the listeners into thinking that KCBQ's commercial load was lower than that of our competitors, which gave the impression that we played more music. A lot of stations used to proclaim that they played "more music," but Buzz turned that overused idea on its head.

He recorded listeners from the request line saying "KCBQ plays *less commercials*." These "drop ins" were played a couple of times an hour. It was a great ploy because people actually began to believe that we did play fewer commercials and much more music than our direct competitor. You've got to hand it to Buzz and Rich Brother, they were genius at the radio game in their time.

Buzz Bennett was program director at KCBQ for exactly one year to the day. On January 4, 1972, corporate headquarters in New York declined his offer to become the national program director for all of their stations, so he resigned. In support of Buzz, Harry Scarborough, the Magic Christian, newsman Ted Tillotson, Rich "Brother" Robbin, Bobby Ocean, Linda and yours truly walked off our jobs.

Looking back, it was a real stupid thing to do. But we all loved Buzz and wanted to support him. We knew someday he would get another job and bring all of us with him. That happened eventually, but it took a while. In the meantime, we all needed to look for a gig.

The first of us who landed one was Bobby Ocean, who hired on as program director of KGB. One of the first things Bobby did was bring his old pal Shotgun Tom on board. So, it was back to Boss Radio for me. Instead of scenic Santee, my daily destination would be the KGB studios at 4141 Pacific Coast Highway, across from the Marine Corps Recruit Depot.

My old pal Wes Owen broke out his movie camera and shot a

documentary of a typical day for me. It shows me leaving my apartment and driving the eerily empty San Diego freeways (this was 1972; the freeways ain't empty these days) in my aquamarine-colored Rambler American. Then I arrive at the station and Wes' camera goes inside to capture me doing my show. I even demonstrate how to "cue-up" a record, something no DJ has done since the digital revolution.

Watch Wes Owen's 1972 documentary on Shotgun Tom at KGB.

Sadly, for me, Boss Radio's days were numbered. In 1972, KGB decided to drop the format and bring in a guy named Ron Jacobs to program the station.

Ironically, Jacobs had been the program director of the biggest Boss Radio station of them all, KHJ 93 in Los Angeles, and was one of the prime movers in launching Casey Kasem's hugely successful syndicated radio show, "American Top 40." But Jacobs wanted no more of Boss Radio or the Top 40.

In April 1972, he produced and broadcast a half-hour radio documentary that ran over and over on KGB non-stop for 24 hours. It chronicled the history of radio leading up to the Top 40/Boss Radio era and then declared that format dead. At the end of the documentary came the announcement that KGB AM and FM were now going to be "recycled." The new format would be a mix of singles and album cuts with mellow, laid-back DJs – a format known as album-oriented rock, or AOR. This just wasn't my thing. I ended up leaving KGB.

My time in the "recycle bin" was pretty short. Buzz Bennett had picked up a station – KRIZ in Phoenix. He offered me the afternoon drive slot and it was off to the Valley of the Sun.

I worked with a lot of great people at KRIZ, including Gerry Cagle, Larry McKay, Jim Nelson and Dave Trout, who later became Freddie Snakeskin on the "World Famous" KROQ in Los Angeles.

I spent the better part of a year in Phoenix. Linda accompanied me there and ended up working in the KRIZ traffic department. Things were going pretty well, but I was homesick for San Diego and KCBQ.

Once again, fate took a hand. KCBQ had a new program director, a really sharp, innovative guy named Jack McCoy.

Jack hired my old Port Hueneme/Bakersfield buddy Dave Conley, and when an opening popped up at the station, Dave put on the full court press for Jack to hire me. Jack offered me the afternoon drive slot at KCBQ. Pretty much a no-brainer.

In a short time, Linda and I were packing our bags ready to head back home to America's Finest City! Linda was able to get a job with the Fotomat Company, based in San Diego, as their assistant media buyer.

Fotomat was a new, innovative company where someone could drive through a kiosk, drop off a roll of film, and then pick up the prints a day later. It was a great opportunity for her to explore the world outside of broadcasting. But even though she worked with radio and TV stations buying airtime, she missed working in a station.

After two years at Fotomat, she was hired at KDEO AM as their traffic manager.

As you'll recall, KDEO played a big part in my early radio adventures. The station was located on Fletcher Parkway in El Cajon, a suburb of San Diego. The building is now home to the Minuteman Press, which, by the way, is the company that printed the cover for this book. Beth and her team are the greatest! In fact, they are my go-to company for all my printing needs, both professional and personal.

Years later, Linda rejoined me at KCBQ, working for Jack McCoy and Doug Herman, who ran a broadcast consulting company funded by KCBQ's corporate headquarters. Their offices were in the back room of the building. Boy! We moved around a lot, but for a number of years we always seemed to end up back "home" at the KCBQ "ranch house" in Santee.

I went back on the air at KCBQ in July 1973 and spent the next three years doing afternoon drive. Jack McCoy managed to make the station sound even more exciting than it had in the Buzz Bennett era.

Along the way he came up with a brilliant idea for a promotion he called "The Last Contest." It generated an unbelievable amount of excitement in San Diego and was later syndicated nationwide. As Ken Levine wrote in a 2015 post on his excellent blog site:

This was ingenious. Every hour the station announced another prize package. And each was unbelievable. 'KCBQ Prize Package #261: Your own Pacific Island, a ninety-foot yacht to get you there, twelve Polynesian girls to attend to your every sexual need, and 12,000,000 tiny umbrellas for tropical drinks.' That sort of thing.

At some point they would give out a phone number. The first person who called it got to choose any prize package he wanted....

Well needless to say, when they did announce the number, they blew out the entire San Diego phone system.

But what was so brilliant about the contest was this: It sounded like they were giving away trillions of dollars. Every conceivable item you wanted – fancy cars, trips, one of the packages included a new house.

Yes, the winning package had to cost a bundle, but not the $7,000,000,000,000,000 it appeared they were giving away. Meanwhile, competing stations gave away movie tickets.

One of my fondest memories of my time at KCBQ is when Linda and I got married. We tied the knot on November 9, 1974 with fellow KCBQ DJ Chuck "Magic" Christian and his wife, Gwen, as our witnesses.

Following the ceremony, Magic and Gwen hosted our wedding reception in their home, with many of our friends in the San Diego broadcast community in attendance. It was a media blast!

Our roster of DJs kept growing. Legendary 93 KHJ Boss jock Charlie Tuna came down to KCBQ to do mornings for a while. When he decided to go back to L.A., Jack hired Philadelphia radio personality Bill Gardner to replace him. Bill and I became very close friends. We even took vacations together. It was so much fun being back at KCBQ in my hometown.

In 1976, Gerry Cagle, who you'll recall I'd known at KRIZ in Phoenix, took over the program director job at KCBQ. Gerry and I got along and he liked my work, so I was doing fine. But Gerry fired my friend Bill Moffitt, who was doing middays. Bill is one of the greatest midday jocks I've ever heard. I just don't know what Gerry was thinking.

Not too long after that, fate took a hand again. In 1976, FM radio was beginning to come into its own. Less expensive, and in some cases portable, FM receivers were finding their way into people's homes and cars. FM stations were trying out new formats like album rock, moving well beyond elevator music and Top 40. Maybe it was time for Top 40 to find its way over to the FM band.

Over at San Diego's KFMB FM, general manager Paul Palmer and program director Bobby Rich were putting together a staff for a Top 40 format on the station, which was going to be rechristened B-100 FM with the slogan, "Better Boogie."

They approached me about doing the morning show and offered me a lot more money than I was making at KCBQ. Even though I didn't really want to leave KCBQ, I decided it was time for a change.

Maybe it was the Moffitt thing, I don't know. I felt I should move on before Gerry Cagle decided I was no longer a hot commodity … so I took the offer.

I handled the morning show on B-100 for four years. Though

not a morning person, I was able to arrive at the station Monday through Friday without too much difficulty. I have to admit, there were times I cut it pretty close, with maybe four minutes (or less) to spare before I signed on. I really had a great time at B-100.

This new San Diego format hit the airwaves with a bang. Soon we were the top-rated FM station in San Diego, and I was very excited to be a part of it. Bobby Rich was a genius at programming the station and had some great innovative programming ideas that brought B-100 to No. 1.

I was so excited to be at B-100 that within a few months of my arrival I took my Super 8 home movie camera with sound and produced a documentary-style film on B-100 starring Paul Palmer, Bobby Rich, and the entire on-air staff. It was this film that inspired Art Vuolo to begin a 45-year career producing in-studio videos of radio personalities across the country.

Watch Shotgun Tom's Super 8 home movie on B-100.

I worked with some incredibly talented air personalities. Among them were Danny Wilde, who later earned his medical degree and became an internist in L.A.; Willie B. Goode; Dr. Boogie (Bobby Rich); Gene Knight; Ken "Beaver Cleaver" Levine, who later went on to become a very successful TV writer and producer; Glen McCartney; Phil Flowers; and Billy Martin, who went back to school and received his degree in

Photo from Irwin Family Archives

The "Better Boogie" Team at B-100-FM

(L to R) Back Row Gene Knight, Kevin Shira, Cherie Sannes, Danny Wilde and Bobby Rich. Front Row Shotgun Tom, Jimmy Rogers and Glen McCartney

family therapy and still practices to this day.

While at B-100, I was nominated and then received the National Air Personality of the Year award from *Billboard* magazine.

Veteran San Diego news reporter Cathy Clark was doing a series on San Diego morning radio shows. She visited my show, letting me talk about my love of the radio business. It's a love that has never died.

Around this time, a couple of life-changing events took place

Photo from Irwin Family Archives

B-100 erected billboards all over the county to promote Shotgun Tom's morning show.

Watch Cathy Clark's 1979 KNSD TV report on Shotgun Tom at B-100.

for us within a few hours. Linda was pregnant, a couple of days away from her due date, and my dad was in the hospital with heart problems. It was a little past midnight on a Sunday morning, and the phone rang. Linda answered. It was the hospital giving us the sad news that dad had passed.

Whether it was the shock of that news or just a coincidence we'll never know, but almost immediately Linda's water broke. We had to put our grief aside and get to the hospital, pronto!

We arrived to find a chaotic scene. There had been a major accident at nearby Cajon Speedway and nurses were being pulled out of the maternity ward and sent to Emergency to handle the injured.

In the early morning hours, it was discovered that our new baby daughter was breech, so they rushed Linda into surgery for an emergency C-section. Quite an eventful Sunday morning for our little family! Fortunately, all went well, and we welcomed our new baby daughter, Melanie Joanne, into the world. She was born at 7:17 the morning of July 10 - 7/10. Coincidently she weighed 7 pounds and 10 ounces.

Our joy as new parents was tempered by the sadness of losing my dad. Had bypass surgery been a more mainstream medical intervention for cardiac disease, that procedure might have saved him. I still miss him and I'm sorry he never got to meet his granddaughter.

The next day, a Monday, the loveliest thing happened. The doctor who had delivered Melanie stopped by Linda's room to check on her. Dr. Merle Naponic knew what had happened to my dad and told Linda he wasn't going to charge us for the delivery. He told Linda to give the money to Melanie and tell her it was from her grandfather.

We invested the money from her delivery and years later she was able use the proceeds as a down payment for a condo. What a lovely act of generosity. I still get choked up thinking about it.

Little did we know years later Melanie would become a labor and delivery nurse working with Dr. Naponic at the same hospital where she was born.

While this was happening, I was on the air at B-100. Linda

had the radio on in her room. As luck or good fortune would have it, this wonderful doctor was still in the room when I came on the air and dedicated a song to our new daughter with a shout-out to the doctor who had delivered her.

I'm glad he got to hear that. The song was Stevie Wonder's "Isn't She Lovely." Melanie sure was - and she still is!

In 1980, after four years at B-100, I received a call from my attorney, Tony Gilliam. "Hey, they don't want to renew your contract - they want to let you go because you appeal to too young of an audience," he told me. "They want to go with an older audience."

Just like that, in the blink of an eye, bye-bye, B-100. I found

Photo from Irwin Family Archives

Shotgun, wife Linda and baby Melanie.

myself jobless, again.

Thankfully, a very short time later I received a call from the general manager of KBZT FM in San Diego, offering me a weekend job doing a jukebox Saturday night request show. At that time, Linda was employed at KPRI FM in the traffic

Photo from Irwin Family Archives

Daddy's boy, Nicholas Irwin.

department. So, between our two jobs we were able to make ends meet.

Not long afterwards, I met Tommy Sablan, who was employed part-time at KBZT. Tommy and I have remained very close over the resulting course of our broadcasting careers. Tommy would go on to produce the renowned "Jeff and Jer Show" that aired for many years on several radio stations in San Diego. Tommy has the distinction of being the only radio producer to be inducted into the National Radio Hall of Fame.

Tommy became my board operator for the jukebox show and worked along with my producer, John Fewel, and Jeff Williams, who was my phone screener. Jeff's father, Jack, was the owner of Pacific Recorders, which made radio control boards and sold them to countless stations across the country. When we first began doing the show, John would ask which guy was Tommy and which one was Jeff. So, to differentiate the two, I would remind John that Jeff was the boy who wore the glasses. Thus, John dubbed Jeff, "The Boy with the Glasses" - a name that stuck over the years.

I truly enjoyed the Saturday Night Jukebox show because I was given total control over what I played, a novelty in radio programming. I also loved receiving and playing requests from my listeners. One was a very talented San Diego radio personality, Jim McInnes. He and his wife Sandi, who also worked in the broadcasting industry, loved to call in and request their favorite oldies for Saturday night poker parties.

During this time, to supplement my income, I took a position at a local San Diego television station, KUSI-TV Channel 51, as booth announcer, a position that consisted of recording all their promos for upcoming shows, as well as station ID's. The guy who wrote the copy for me was Frank Forth, who later became the audio guy for red carpet interviews for the Oscars.

One Saturday night, Frank decided to visit our show at KBZT. During the show, Frank thought he was having a heart attack, so the paramedics were called. We laid Frank on the floor and since we didn't have a blanket, John Fewel covered him with his jacket. When the paramedics arrived, John removed his jacket and a bag of John's marijuana fell out of the jacket pocket onto Frank's chest. As John was quickly grabbing the bag of weed, he caught the paramedic's eye. The paramedic gave John a sly smile but said nothing. At that time, marijuana was illegal and a potential felony offense. What a close call for John.

By the way, Frank was just having an anxiety attack.

Mark Larson from KFMB AM was very impressed with the show. He thought it would be a great fit on his station. He called and offered me a deal. Not only would I broadcast on Saturday nights, but also Sundays as well. What really sealed the deal was that I could change the name to "Shotgun Tom's Jukebox." How could I resist?

At the same time, a new Fifties-themed restaurant called the Corvette Diner opened up in Hillcrest. It was extremely popular. Their menu included a wide range of "diner foods," hamburgers, fries, meatloaf, shakes, malts and more. You name it, they served it.

My family and I were having lunch there one Saturday. David Cohn, the owner, recognized me and came over and ended up chatting with us for over an hour. We discussed my Shotgun Tom's Jukebox show and I told him how much I loved playing the oldies, especially focusing on requests from my listeners.

Then David came up with a fabulous idea."Why don't you do the show live from my restaurant every Saturday and Sunday night?" He asked. "You'll be able to take requests not only from the radio listeners, but also the customers. The patrons will be able to hear their requests played while they're dining. I'll even build you a studio."

How could I turn that offer down? Doing my show and interacting with my listeners, all from a picture window

Photo from Irwin Family Archives

Shotgun Tom broadcasting live from the Corvette Diner.

studio? Talk about dreams come true!

David was true to his word. He contacted KFMB Radio and they struck a deal. He built a picture window studio in the corner of the restaurant. That's where I did my show for the next seven years.

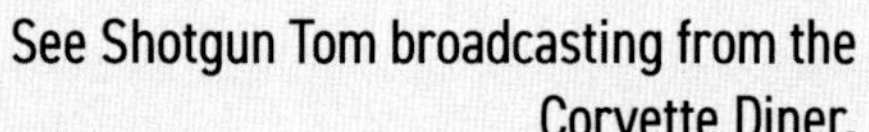
See Shotgun Tom broadcasting from the Corvette Diner.

I absolutely loved every minute of it. Since then, David Cohn and his wife, Leslie, have become a true San Diego success story. Beginning with one small diner in 1981, Cohn Restaurant Group now owns and operates 25 restaurants throughout Southern California and Maui.

By the way, the Corvette Diner still exists, but has moved from its original location on 5th Avenue in Hillcrest to Liberty Station off Rosecrans Street in Point Loma. Liberty Station was the former home of the San Diego Naval Training Center. When the training center closed its doors, it was developed into a prosperous shopping and dining center. The Corvette Diner still features the announcer's booth on site that continues to be used to this day by various other DJs. Even though I don't make any more appearances, several pictures of me are featured with a clock that reads "Shotgun Tom's Jukebox."

While I was working at KFMB AM, I had the great opportunity to meet one of my favorite recording artists, Johnny Mathis.

My very good friend, Bill Martin, and I attended the San Diego Pops concert featuring Mr. Mathis. We both wanted to meet him, very much so, and came up with a great idea about a way to make it happen.

You may recall one of the first radio personalities Bill and I personally knew was Frank Thompson from KOGO AM Radio. By then, Frank had left San Diego and was now the news director at KJR AM in Seattle. It just so happened that he and Johnny Mathis were well acquainted. So, as bold as I can be at times, I wrote a note introducing Bill and myself to Johnny, mentioning that we were great friends of Frank Thompson and would love the pleasure of meeting him. Then Bill and I went to the entrance to the backstage area, and I asked the guard to please hand the note to Johnny.

Neither Bill nor I really expected Johnny to respond, but we held high hopes. A few minutes later, much to our surprise, the backstage door flung open and there was Johnny, beckoning us in.

Johnny could not have been more cordial. He had lost contact with Frank and was anxious to hear his whereabouts. He also wanted to hear all about how we met Frank and our present careers and so on. The kinds of questions a true friend would ask.

As we were leaving, he asked for Frank's current information. Soon we heard that Johnny had contacted Frank and arranged to fly him down to Johnny's Hollywood home and entertain him for a week.

Coincidentally, I found out that Johnny's home engineer was a good friend of mine, Frank Martin. To this day, he is still employed by Johnny. I also kept in touch with Johnny, and I've been a welcome guest in his home over the years.

After I'd been at KUSI-TV about a year, the owner of the station, Mike McKinnon, came up to me. "You worked over at Channel 10 hosting a kids show, so since you have experience with kids shows, I'd like you to host a daily children's show at KUSI TV. We're going to call it the 'KUSI Kids Club.'"

"What kids show on Channel 10?" you ask. Well, maybe it's time for me to step out of the jock booth and tell you a little about my television adventures.

Words-A-Poppin' & Annoying Jerry Lewis

As mentioned earlier, I had always been interested in getting into children's television, in addition to my radio career. My interest dated back to many years before I became a parent.

I also took note of how television work enhanced the careers of some DJs in a big way. Gary Owens on "Laugh-In", Bob Eubanks on "The Newlywed Game" and Wink Martindale on TV game shows such as "Gambit" and "Tic-Tac-Dough" are a few examples of local LA DJs who established names for themselves nationally on TV.

For my part, I'd already dipped my toe in the water as Nemo the Clown in Bakersfield. I wondered if I could do something similar in San Diego.

I decided to approach the same station where I'd watched Johnny Downs when I was a kid, KOGO Channel 10. The new station owners, McGraw-Hill, had changed the call letters to

KGTV. I made an appointment to meet program director Phil Corvo.

I pitched Phil on the idea of hosting cartoons, but he quickly told me that kind of show was history. Phil said that, inspired by PBS' "Sesame Street," he was looking to produce an educational children's show that would hopefully satisfy the station's FCC requirements for educational children's programming, while still pulling in good ratings.

He had come up with a game show idea that would help kids enhance their vocabularies. The show would be called "Words-A-Poppin,'" and Phil was looking for a show host. He invited me to audition.

A week later, I showed up at Channel 10. About 20 aspiring TV hosts were sequestered in the station cafeteria. One of them I recognized immediately. It was Johnny Downs, the host I'd watched as a kid!

Without hesitation, I walked up to him. "Johnny, it's so wonderful to meet you," I said, barely containing my excitement. "I'm Shotgun Tom Kelly and you're one of my all-time great television heroes! I have no chance of winning this audition. I'm going to be watching you every Saturday on 'Words-A-Poppin.' It'll be so great to see you back on TV again!"

I must have sounded like I was shot out of a cannon. Johnny told me to calm down. He took the lid off a thermos he was carrying, poured us a cup of coffee, and said, "You have as much right to audition for the show as I do. Drink your coffee and relax."

Johnny auditioned before I did. As he walked out of the studio he said, "Good luck, Shotgun, you will do great!" and walked out of the station.

I walked into the studio and kids on the set knew who I was. I could hear them whispering, "Shotgun Tom from KCBQ!" Then I was introduced to director Dempsey Copeland and producer Carol Nafie.

The show consisted of two teams of three kids competing in games called Mix a Word, Build a Word and Find a Word. After I was done, Dempsey and Carole said, "Good job! We will call you." I didn't hear from anybody for four weeks, so I assumed that Johnny Downs got the job.

Then one day, Dempsey Copeland called me at KCBQ and said they'd made their decision: I would be host of "Words-A-Poppin'." "No, that can't be! Johnny Downs has more experience," I said, not hiding my disbelief. "He should've gotten the job, don't you think?"

Dempsey responded by saying the kids related more to me than Johnny, or anybody else. "We want to start production in the next week," he added.

Things started happening fast. Dempsey said he wanted my hair and beard reined in a bit and sent me to a barber named Kirby Winn. An appointment was made for me with the station makeup department, where I learned about pancake makeup and how to apply it.

Once we took care of those on-camera appearance details, Producer Carol Nafie gave me five scripts for the first five

Photo from Irwin Family Archives

Shotgun Tom, dressed to the nines
for his gig hosting "Words-A-Poppin'."

shows. We were going to tape on Saturdays. Three shows would be taped back-to-back on Saturday morning, followed by a break for lunch, and then two more show tapings in the afternoon. They would bring in a different audience for each show. We were going to shoot a total of 25 shows, which would comprise a season.

Watch a clip of Shotgun Tom
hosting "Words-A-Poppin'."

Our crew included a great floor director, Fred Bushardt Jr., and a great announcer, Mike Ambrose, a former KDEO DJ who at the time was the highly popular weather man at Channel 10. My ace in the hole was my wife, Linda, who drilled me on all the words. We went over all of the scripts the week before I was to shoot each Saturday.

What I didn't realize was they wanted to syndicate the show to all the McGraw-Hill stations around the country! The stations included KMGH TV in Denver, WRTV in Indianapolis and KERO TV in Bakersfield (where years before I was Nemo the Clown) and KGTV San Diego, of course.

Photo from Irwin Family Archives

Shotgun Tom with the "Words-A-Poppin'" crew.

One embarrassing gaffe happened during one of the "Words-A-Poppin'" tapings in front of a live audience. During one of the games, Bob Bound, the guy who handled the letters backstage, slipped in an incorrect letter. The producer really let him have it. She was so loud I could hear her through the floor director's headset! We had to stop and reset, which gave me a chance to walk backstage and console poor Bob. However, I forgot that I still had my lavalier mic on, clipped to my tie. One of the first things they teach you in broadcasting is to treat a microphone like a gun. Always assume a gun is loaded. Always assume a mic is hot. On the radio, it's easy to remember that, with a big silver RCA 77 DX staring you in the face. But one of those tiny lavalier mics clipped to your tie is easy to forget.

Unfortunately, I forgot. Even more unfortunately, the sound guy hadn't turned my mic off. Everything I said would boom into the sound stage.

Once I got backstage, I ran up to Bob. "Don't worry about it, Bob! It's no big deal. They can just go piss up a rope!" Every word of that went onto the soundstage, loud and clear. The audience heard every word as well … and so did Linda. There were murmurs in the audience: "This is outrageous! Doesn't he know children are present?"

Linda leapt out of her seat and ran backstage. She pointed at my tie and whispered, "Your mic is hot! They can hear you out there."

Man, did I feel like an idiot! Luckily, a few minutes later we were able to start taping again, and everything went smoothly from that point on without me taking too much grief. As you might imagine, I learned my lesson about lavalier mics.

We enjoyed a wonderful five-year run with "Words-A-Poppin'," during which I won two Emmy Awards as the host.

Photo from Irwin Family Archives

Shotgun Tom won two Emmy Awards
as host of "Words-A-Poppin'."

My first two ventures into television worked out quite well, as Nemo the Clown and as the "Words-A-Poppin'" host. Why not keep a good thing going?

With that, I moved into my next foray into television. In 1973, Dick Alderson, the San Diego director of the Muscular Dystrophy Association, approached me about being a cohost on the "Jerry Lewis Labor Day Telethon" on Channel 10 and becoming a carnival chairman for MDA backyard carnivals. I decided to accept his gracious invitation.

Starting in 1966, comedian Jerry Lewis had begun hosting a 20-plus-hour-long telethon over the Labor Day weekend to raise money in the fight against muscular dystrophy. The show originated in Las Vegas and was broadcast on a network of stations.

Periodically throughout the telecast, Lewis would take a break and throw it to the local stations, where local hosts would continue the fund raising. That would be my job.

Every year, the Muscular Dystrophy Association would have a meeting in Las Vegas at the Sahara hotel with Jerry Lewis and the local MDA hosts. We would have our picture taken with Jerry, for promotional purposes at the various stations around the country. You stepped in line, walked up to Jerry, smiled and they took the picture. That was that. No introduction.

About five years into my MDA co-hosting career, I was at one of these meetings at the Sahara in Vegas riding down on the elevator. The elevator stopped, the door opened and in walked Jerry Lewis carrying his golf clubs.

Photo from Irwin Family Archives

Shotgun Tom with Jerry Lewis.

Before we go on, I need to hit the pause button and give you a little background. In 1946, a 19-year-old Jerry Lewis teamed up with a handsome 27-year-old crooner named Dean Martin. It was only supposed to be for one appearance, but the chemistry between the two of them was nothing short of dynamic and fetching. They began appearing as Martin and Lewis and by 1951, they were playing the biggest showrooms in Las Vegas, which was rapidly growing into America's favorite adult playground and entertainment center, as well as the hottest supper clubs around the country. Martin and Lewis co-hosted a radio show, they made record albums, they co-starred on television, and they made movies. By 1951, they were the highest paid act in show business, according to *Life* magazine: The hottest of rising stars.

Five years later, in 1956, it was over. What caused their

breakup? No one ever said. There was endless speculation, but nobody seemed to know for sure.

One theory, according to a *People* magazine article, is that Dean Martin began to feel that Jerry Lewis was exercising too much control over their work and wanted to go back to being a solo act. Lewis, who still worshipped Martin, felt betrayed, and the two soon stopped speaking. One thing that was certain was that they felt tremendous bitterness that went both ways. It would be many years before the two even spoke to each other again.

I didn't really know any of this. I knew they'd been a comedy team, but at the time they split up, I was just a little kid. Martin and Lewis were of my parents' generation, and so not on my radar. One of the reasons I knew they had been a team was because one of my prize possessions was a tape someone gave me of the outtakes from a Martin and Lewis recording session.

On the tape, they recorded a radio commercial, as only the two great entertainers could, for a movie they'd just made called *The Caddy*. There's plenty of goofing around, fluffing of lines and a lot of profanity – mostly from Lewis. I used to listen to that tape and crack up. I'd play it for friends and they'd crack up, too.

Now, back to the action. I decided to make small talk in the elevator with Jerry. I introduced myself and explained that we raised a lot of money in San Diego for the MDA backyard carnival program. Lewis looked at me with flat eyes and no expression, really bored.

It was obvious he thought I was some kind of a nut and he

just wanted to get out of the elevator. Drowning in flop-sweat, I started talking about the *Caddy* outtake tape, not realizing that the last thing Jerry wanted to hear about was his days with Dean! Jerry glared at me and then screamed at the top of his lungs, "I don't want to talk about it!"

The elevator stopped, the door opened and in walked Bob Ross, Jerry's manager. "What's going on?" asked Bob. Jerry glared at him and again screamed, "I don't want to talk about it!!!"

Mercifully, the elevator reached the ground floor. Lewis grabbed his golf bag and was gone. I walked back up to our room and told Linda, "I just pissed off Jerry Lewis in the elevator."

Unfortunately, following my encounter, we had to attend a lunch meeting with all the other cohosts from around the country. Jerry, up on the dais, looked down at our table and spotted me. He stepped off the dais and was walking toward our table.

I turned to Linda. "Oh man, I'm in trouble now! Jerry is gonna throw us out of here!"

When Lewis arrived at my table, something quite different happened. "Shotgun, I want to apologize for what happened in the elevator today," he said.

Wow ... and, he'd remembered my name!

"You brought up a very sensitive topic, something I don't like to think about. Please forgive me."

Then he gave me a big Hollywood hug.

Every year afterward, when I stood in line with the other cohosts to get our new photos taken for the MDA Telethon, Jerry would say, "Well, here comes Shotgun Tom! Are you going to start something again?"
Oh no, sir!

I continued to host the annual Muscular Dystrophy Telethon for 24 years in San Diego and 14 years in Los Angeles.

Some of my other TV work involved hosting a Saturday show called "Disco 10" on KGTV, featuring kids from high schools all over San Diego. The show was produced by Doug Rose.

It was a dance show, mirroring The Real Don Steele's Los Angeles TV show that aired during the Sixties. I also filled in

Photo from Irwin Family Archives

I even got to work with Casey Kasem!

Photo from Irwin Family Archives

Shotgun Tom on the MDA Telethon, KCAL 9 Los Angeles.

for "Words-A-Poppin'" announcer Mike Ambrose doing the weather during Channel 10 news.

Back to the "KUSI Kids Club." The show was produced by Barbara Ayres and then Linda Helseth. It aired in the mornings and again in the afternoons. The show consisted

Photo from Irwin Family Archives

Shotgun Tom hosting the "KUSI Kids Club."

of featured cartoons and prize giveaways, which I would do during the breaks.

Often, we did remote broadcasts from various places throughout San Diego, like the San Diego Zoo and Sea World. We would invite the kids to our remotes and tape segments for later airing.

On one occasion, Disney sent a rep down to San Diego to appear on the "Kids Club" promoting the movie *The Little*

Watch Shotgun Tom hosting the "KUSI Kids Club."

Mermaid. It was highly successful, and I like to think I helped with that success.

A few times I brought in my pal Russ T. Nailz, a very talented local comedian, performer and musician, to entertain the kids on the set. The kids loved his ability to relate to them. As he entertained them with his songs, he would soon have them singing along. Shows were always fun with Russ T. Nailz on board!

During the Eighties, there were only a few TV channels to watch, so our competition was low. We were the only game in town catering to local kid's programming, other than Uncle Murph on XETV-6.

Which probably explains why, to this day, I have people coming up to me saying they remember me from the "KUSI Kids Club." These 30- and 40-year-olds spent their youth watching our show before and after school, and it became a big part of their day. I hosted the show Mondays through Fridays for over 12 years.

See Shotgun Tom on KGTV ABC 10's "Disco 10" show.

New York, Here I (Almost) Come

Around 1980, fellow broadcaster and very dear friend Big Ron O'Brien and I were approached and asked to audition for a new upcoming TV channel. We weren't told much about the concept except that they wanted us to introduce music videos.

As broadcasters always looking for any new gig around any corner, we traveled up to L.A. for our audition. The producer was Bob Pittman (now chairman and CEO of iHeart Media). He seemed to approve of our act and asked us for a call back session. So, we obliged. The only caveat was that we would have to move to New York.

Even though the thought of leaving San Diego did not quite appeal to me, it sounded like it might be a great opportunity. Unfortunately, or maybe not, neither Ron nor I made the second cut. I wasn't too heartbroken, since I wanted to continue to stay in San Diego broadcasting and had no idea what type of a show the producers had in mind or if it would even take off.

Well, it took off. Did it ever! The channel for which we auditioned turned out to be none other than MTV, which changed the face of music and music videos when it debuted on August 1, 1981.

KBZT, And Then On To Modern Oldies

In the early Nineties, Rich Brother Robbin became the program director of KBZT FM in San Diego. He hired me to be the afternoon drive jock. I was surrounded by many talented broadcasters such as "Crazy" Dave Smith (who later became the entertainment director for the San Diego Zoo and Safari Park), Ken Copper and Dayle Ohlau. I really enjoyed working afternoons, playing the oldies. But Rich Brother (very ahead of his time) had developed a new format he wanted to implement. He named it *modern oldies*, which is very much like the current extremely successful *classic hits* format.

Unfortunately, KBZT FM wasn't interested in Rich's innovative idea, so Rich searched around and found a radio station that was willing to implement the format. KCBQ FM, the FM counterpart to the AM Top 40 station I had been at earlier in my career, gave Rich a shot. Truthfully, I was very content playing the oldies at KBZT. But the very persuasive Rich talked me into going "across the street" with him. I was hired for the afternoon drive.

Rich decided to bring in several talents with whom he had worked in Tucson, along with other air personalities to round out the staff. I was surrounded by a group of guys I had never worked with, or, for that matter, never heard of like Royce Blake, Jeff Stewart, Nixon Lowe, Mike Esparza, and The Goat Boy.

Soon Eddie Pappani (who would later become the very successful morning drive host of "The Show" on iHeart's Rock 105.3 FM in San Diego) and Mark Jagger (known for hosting mornings at Local Media San Diego's Magic 92.5 with his wife Kristi) became members of our "modern oldies" team. I found that I enjoyed working with all of the staff; I keep in touch with some of them to this day. In fact, Eddie Pappani and I are recurring guests on the local TV show "On the Air" with Sully and Little Tommy (Sablan). More about "On the Air" later in the book, so keep reading.

A Strange, Sad Detour

One Sunday in June 1985, the body of a young woman named Donna Gentile was discovered on Sunrise Highway, 30 miles northeast of San Diego in the Laguna Mountains.

She had been brutally murdered.

Just 22 years old, Donna struggled through a short, unhappy life which ended with her working as a prostitute. Five weeks before her death, she had testified at a Civil Service hearing, implicating two San Diego police officers in a prostitution scandal. You might well wonder how I could have any connection to this poor young woman's tragic tale. Buckle up. It's quite a story.

Nowadays I'm all about model trains, but back in the early Eighties my hobby was video. Home video gear was now available, and I bought a bunch of it. I used it to amuse my family and friends by producing my version of NBC's

"Tonight Show" in my garage. I built a whole "Tonight Show" set, complete with a desk, couch, chair, backdrop and even curtains as background for the monologues. The only missing element was the canned theme music.

At that time, my friend David Shields, a songwriter and producer, was recording a jingle session. David said he could piggyback my session with his. He had a full orchestra and allowed me 13 cuts, including my own custom-made "Tonight Show" theme. David was able to give me a fabulous deal. For $3,000, the orchestra would record all my theme music.

Well, I went for it. I was there in the control room, looking through the window at a full orchestra, ready to record. I could see the sax section, the percussion, the trumpets, and Dave as he played the piano and directed the orchestra. It was a dream come true. It was absolutely amazing that all 13 cuts were done in just one take.

My friends became my volunteer TV crew. One of them, Bill Moffitt, was my audio engineer. He held that role during all of my "Tonight" shows. We recorded about 29 episodes with a variety of hosts and guests.

Two of the most notable were Hollywood movie and TV script writers Ken Levine – the same Ken Levine who wrote my speech when I got the star on the Hollywood Walk of Fame – and his partner, David Isaacs. They recorded the show long before they became successful. We were all blown away by their talent and knew they were destined to make it big in Hollywood.

And, of course, they did. They've written scripts for "The

Jeffersons," "M*A*S*H," "Cheers," and "The Simpsons," just to name a few.

Some of my other guest hosts included family members, former NFL football player Kellen Winslow, Heisman Trophy winner Johnny Rodgers, and Pat Curran. Following Pat's football career, he became the color analyst on the San Diego Chargers' radio broadcast with Jim Laslavic. Pat was also the business manager for the Chargers. Also, many of my broadcast colleagues were featured, including Chuck "The Chucker" Browning, Dave Conley, Jack McCoy, Big Ron O'Brian, Jack Vincent, Big John Carter, and voice actor Neil Ross, who (by the way) helped me write this book.

Neil is very well known in the voiceover industry. He is the voice of countless cartoon characters, such as Shipwreck on "GI Joe." He was also the live announcer for the Academy Awards.

Years later, while watching an episode of "Seinfeld," I was dumbstruck to see that the character Kramer had constructed a late-night show set in his living room!

Today, when people view my recorded shows, they always say, "Oh, so you got the idea from Kramer on 'Seinfeld'?" I proceed to set them straight and tell them that my "Tonight Show" was produced long before "Seinfeld" was even a series.

One of my most famous shows featured San Diego County Sheriff John Duffy and San Diego Police Chief Bill Kolender. The show was a total success and a cult favorite. For seven years, the video tapes were passed around among people in law enforcement. Both the Sheriff's Department and the San

Diego Police Department knew about this TV show. It was no secret.

Around this time, a homicide task force was formed to investigate a number of murders that seemed to have a common thread. The unsolved murders of 43 prostitutes in the San Diego area took place over a time span of 10 years. The task force was created to take the investigation out of the hands of the San Diego Sheriff and Police departments because of allegations that some of their personnel might have been involved.

As they reviewed individual cases, the task force found itself focusing on the recent killing of Donna Gentile. There was speculation that the killer might have been a cop.

Here's where it gets weird. The task force came across an informant who told them that Donna Gentile had appeared on the John Duffy/Bill Kolender show, which was taped in my garage! Where and why this guy came up with this ridiculous story, I have no idea.

I was unaware of this, so when I received a call from the task force investigators asking to visit me in my home to see the show, I had no qualms and happily obliged. To say the least, the investigators were very entertained by Sheriff John Duffy's monologue.

Then, they became a little more serious and began showing me some photos of a fundraising event. The first picture was a friend of mine, business owner Johnny Helmer. Next, they showed me a second photo of another very good friend of mine, Tuxedo Store owner Jerry Klein. Then they asked if I had attended that event.

"Yes," I said.

Then they showed me the third picture and there I was, front and center. They were trying to catch me in a lie. I should have realized at that time that they were a little more serious about any involvement I may have had with their investigation. But they appeared satisfied and left without comment.

A couple of weeks after the detective's visit, my wife Linda, my two children and I attended my niece's wedding in San Francisco. While we were in our hotel room preparing for the wedding festivities, one of our neighbors called to let us know the task force was at our house.

Luckily, my neighbors, Jerry Howe and John Dukes, were home that day and happened to see multiple cop cars in front of my house. They asked to see the search warrant and when they realized that all was in order, they told the investigators that they had a key to our house, so there was no need for the police to break down the door.

The task force took away 750 of my video tapes, including the Kolender/Duffy "Tonight Show." The warrant said detectives were trying to find images of murder victim Donna Gentile and "any person who could be suspected of being a prostitute."

I later learned they confronted the informant, and rather than admit he'd made the whole thing up, he'd doubled down and told the detectives they'd only seen an edited version of the show. He assured them that there was an X-rated version, with Donna Gentile featured, hidden in my house.

And the task force bought his story!

I must add that even though the task force looked in every drawer and cabinet in our home, they left everything in pristine order.

Nothing was out of place, except one oddity. On our bed they placed one of my signature Ranger hats and a photo of me and Sheriff John Duffy taken on my "Tonight Show" set. Very chilling. In fact, Linda and I worried that our house might be bugged!

The story made the rounds on all of the major San Diego television stations: KNSD, NBC 7/39 and KFMB TV CBS-8. My good friend, local NBC anchor Marty Levin, informed me that reporters were attempting to track me down. He was kind enough to actually let me know their exact whereabouts, especially when they were posted in front of my house.

I gave an interview to Paul Bloom on his KNSD TV crime watch. He was very fair, asking before the cameras rolled; "Shotgun, is this a publicity stunt?" I assured him nobody wants that kind of press.

Paul filmed the report at my garage "Tonight Show" set. At the end, he said, "I just talked to Shotgun Tom and he said there's nothing on the tape that will interest the homicide task force." Then he tossed it to news anchor Levin. Marty asked Paul if he had talked with Police Chief Bill Kolender or John Duffy. Paul said he had, and they were happily handing out tapes for everybody to see for themselves.

The *San Diego Evening Tribune* gave the story front page news above the fold. The story was even reported as far north as Los Angeles. My friend Neil Ross, up in Manhattan Beach, spat his cornflakes halfway across the breakfast table when he read it in the L.A. papers. I always wanted to be on the front page, but not like this!

Copyright 1990 San Diego Tribune

SAN DIEGO TRIBUNE WEEKEND

San Diego's Pulitzer Prize-winning Newspaper — Saturday, September 8, 1990 — 25 Cents — A Copley Newspaper

Task force seizes 750 videos in murder probe

The San Diego Metropolitan Homicide Task Force seized about 750 videotapes from a local broadcast personality, looking for clues to the murders of 43 women, Sheriff John Duffy has confirmed.

Duffy made the statement to a San Diego Tribune reporter in response to questions about allegations that Duffy had appeared in a videotape with slain prostitute Donna Gentile. People interviewed by the task force have told the Tribune that investigators asked them about a single recording that might contain the images of Gentile, Duffy and former Police Chief Bill Kolender.

Kolender and Duffy deny even knowing Gentile, let alone appearing in a videotape with her.

"There has never been any videotape in existence that portrays Bill Kolender, Donna Gentile and John Duffy," Duffy said. "Anybody who says that should be quite careful, and any newspaper who prints it should be quite careful about what they print."

Duffy said the task force review of the tapes turned up no such recording

This story was produced by Tribune staff writers David Hasemyer, Eddy McNeil, Rick Shaughnessy and Mark T. Sullivan

and, furthermore, he denied that finding such a tape was the purpose of the seizure. He refused to elaborate.

Bonnie Dumanis, a deputy district attorney who serves as the task force spokeswoman, would not confirm or deny that investigators are looking for a tape involving Kolender, Duffy and Gentile.

But 10 people interviewed by the San Diego Tribune said they either believe such a tape existed or were questioned by task force detectives about such a tape. None said they had firsthand knowledge of such a tape.

If such a tape existed, it would be the first concrete link between top law-enforcement officials and Gentile, a streetwalker who spoke out against two police officers and was found dead a month after one of them was fired.

That was in 1985. Since then 42 more women, mostly prostitutes and drug users, have been found slain and abandoned in San Diego County. Their deaths are being investigated by the task force, a cooperative unit formed by the San Diego Police Department, the Sheriff's Department and the district attorney's office two years ago.

The 750 tapes were seized four weeks ago from the El Cajon home of Thomas J. Irwin, a local radio and television personality widely known as Shotgun Tom Kelly. He is a free-lancer who has hosted a children's entertainment show on KUSI-TV, among other jobs.

Irwin makes videotapes both as a hobby and as a business. The garage of his home is converted into a variety/talk-show set patterned after NBC-TV's "The Tonight Show."

There, Irwin estimates, he has produced about 20 videotaped variety

Please see TAPES, A-4, Col. 1

Former Police Chief Bill Kolender, left, and Sheriff John Duffy exchange a laugh during the videotaping of "The Sheriff John Duffy Show." The variety show, patterned after NBC's "The Tonight Show," was filmed in 1984. The photograph was made from a copy of the videotape.

The incident cast a shadow over my entire career. At that time, I was hosting a children's show on KUSI TV. The owner, Mike McKinnon, took me off the air for three days. My wife Linda, who at the time was the PTA president at Fletcher Hills Elementary School, was understandably very upset. I hired an attorney, George Manning, to represent me and help clear my name.

The 750 tapes seized from my house contained more than 4,500 hours of video on them, which some poor task force investigator had to sit and watch.

What a waste of manpower! Finally, the task force concluded that there was no other "dirty" version of the tape. They admitted to the press that my house should never have been raided. I was exonerated.

Still, to this day there are some who wonder if perhaps I did have another version of that infamous "Tonight Show" tape.

Which is why, at this time, I would like to state that there is only one version of the John Duffy/Kolender "Tonight Show." And Donna Gentile ain't in it.

As of this writing, the murder of Donna Gentile has never been solved. I feel so sorry for that poor girl and for her family. In no way did she deserve such a tragic fate.

May God rest her soul.

Watch a KNSD TV report on the raid on Shotgun Tom's house.

Talkin' Mics With The Prez

It was 1983. I was working weekends at KFMB AM, broadcasting live from the Corvette Diner. During the week I was hosting the KUSI "Kid's Club" program.

Congressman Duncan L. Hunter asked for my help on a radio commercial he was working on. I enlisted the aid of KFMB production director Tony Pepper and together we came up with an ad that really pleased the congressman.

He thanked me profusely and asked how he could repay me. I didn't hesitate for a moment. "Duncan," I said, "I'd like to meet President Reagan."

You recall my story earlier in this book about my dad meeting then-President Truman? Well, I wanted to meet a president, too.

Duncan said he thought he could make that happen. As fate would have it, Ronald

Reagan was scheduled to hold a rally in San Diego, and the congressman invited me to serve as emcee!

Ronald Reagan had always considered San Diego to be his lucky city, and one of his final campaign speeches on his re-election campaign tour was going to be held in Fashion Valley. I told Duncan that I'd be thrilled to do it.

A couple of months later, I stood on the presidential podium, introducing Charlton Heston, Robert Stack, and Wayne Newton. I was there for about four hours welcoming and introducing various dignitaries as we awaited the landing of Air Force One and the motorcade that would bring the president to the event.

Finally the motorcade arrived backstage and out of the Presidential car they called "The Beast" emerged President Reagan, his wife, Nancy, and Frank Sinatra.

The White House staffer turned to me and said, "Shotgun, thank you so much for doing a great job. Please stand behind the red rope area. We have a recording that introduces President Reagan."

Well, there I was off the podium behind the red rope with Police Chief Bill Kolender. I said, "Bill, you've got to do something. I need to get back up there and meet the president and say hello to Frank Sinatra. And possibly get our picture taken."

Bill proceeded to tell me that he had no jurisdiction and he pointed to the guy with his hand on a briefcase. Bill said, "That's a Secret Service agent, and he has his trigger finger on an Uzi. If we cross this red rope line, he'll shoot first and ask questions later."

Meanwhile, Duncan Hunter noticed I was off the podium behind the red rope and kept motioning to me to get back up on stage. But all I could think about was that Uzi, so I stayed put and missed my chance to meet the president.

Duncan, however, was determined to make it happen. A few weeks later, he got in touch. "Why don't I arrange for you to come to the White House and present one of your trademark ranger hats to the president in the oval office?"

"That would be perfect," I said.

Almost a year later, I was at the KUSI television studios hosting the live breaks on camera. I walked out to the station lobby and saw a message for me from Duncan Hunter: "Your appointment with the President has been approved."

I was so excited! After my broadcast at KUSI TV, I went over to see my friend Tony Pepper in the production room at KFMB radio and told him my good news. He grabbed me by the collar and yanked me into a studio where nobody could hear us. "Don't tell anybody about this," Tony said, his voice a warning.

"There are people at this station who are going to be jealous and feel like they're more entitled to meet the president than you. Don't tell anybody!" I heeded Tony's sage advice and maintained radio silence.

A week later, I hopped on a plane and flew to Washington

D.C. I landed about 10 a.m., checked into my hotel room, put on my suit and took a cab over to the Cannon Building, where Duncan Hunter's office was located. Our appointment to see the president in the Oval Office at the White House was at 4:30 p.m.

I got to Duncan's office around 11 a.m. I sat down in a chair, and I felt a tear in the seat of my suit pants. I hadn't worn that suit in a couple of years, and I guess I'd put on a pound or three.

Duncan said, "Don't worry. I'll have one of my aides sew it up for you."

I went into his office, took my pants off and gave them to him. "Here, sit in my chair," the congressman said. "I've got to go over and cast a vote in the House and then I'll come back, and we'll go to lunch with my son, Duncan Jr."

I sat in the congressman's chair behind his desk in my skivvies, waiting for my pants to get sewn up and for the congressman to return. Then we went over to the congressional dining room and had lunch with Duncan and 6-year-old Duncan Hunter Jr.

After lunch, the congressman again had to go over and cast a vote on the floor of the House of Representatives. While he was gone, he asked me to babysit Duncan Jr. I happily obliged.

After the vote, we walked over to his office in the Cannon building. His wife was there and took Duncan Jr. home.

By now, it was about 3 p.m. We got in Duncan's car which, by the way, needed some work done because the passenger door had to be held shut with a rope.

Were WE a pair; me with my split pants, him with a car door that needed a rope to close!

When we arrived at the White House, the Secret Service took a look at this beater car, and were probably thinking about drawing their guns.

Fortunately, they quickly identified Duncan and it was smooth sailing from that point on. I asked Duncan if he was ever going to get the door fixed. "If my constituents can't afford to get their cars fixed, I can't afford to get mine fixed," he replied.

We parked the car and walked into the White House. The Secret Service gave us our White House visitor passes and Duncan said to just put it under my shirt.

My pass had a chip in it so the Secret Service could see where I was at all times.

The President was meeting five people in the Oval Office that day. They included a former Miss America, Duncan Hunter, another congressman, a senator, and me. I was obviously in good company.

They took us to the cabinet room next to the Oval Office. There, one by one, we were led into a small hallway, just outside the Oval Office.

Finally, the White House staff personnel said, "Mr. Hunter, Mr. Kelly, it's your turn to meet the President."

In we walked, me wearing my trademark ranger hat and carrying another ranger hat that I was going to present to Mr. Reagan.

The president was behind the Resolute Desk, a double pedestal desk made from the oak timbers of a British ship, the HMS Resolute. The desk had been gifted in 1880 to President Rutherford B. Hayes by Queen Victoria. President Reagan got up and walked over to the nearby shell bookcase. The president had been briefed about my appearance in the room.

"Well, Shotgun, I understand that you were the emcee and kept the people entertained while they were waiting for me in San Diego," President Reagan said.

I said, "Yes, Mr. President, I did, and I bring you my trademark ranger hat and I hope you'll put it on."

"Well..." and then he put it on. That's when the White House photographer took the photo of me and the president in our matching ranger hats.

I had seen the Oval Office on TV many times, but in person, I realized that it was a lot smaller than I had thought. There was a fireplace at one end and the Resolute Desk at the other. Two couches and a coffee table sat atop the presidential seal etched into the carpet.

Within moments, the President and I got into a conversation about broadcasting. Mr. Reagan said, "You know, I used to be in radio. My job was to re-create the baseball games at the station while the team was out of town because the station couldn't afford to send the announcers along with the team.

You probably don't remember the days of re-creates."

"Mr. President," I replied, "I do remember, because in my hometown, San Diego, Al Shush, Al Coupe and Tommy Jorgenson would re-create baseball games while the San Diego Padres were out of town."

"Oh, then," said the President, "You know from where I speak."

"Yes, Mr. President, I sure do!"

Then we started talking about microphones from the past, models like the RCA 77 DX ribbon microphone and RCA 44 BX. Then Mr. Reagan told me that when he was at Paramount Studios, there was a makeup guy whose name was Shotgun.

I found myself thinking about all the amazing people who had been in the Oval Office over the years, the crises they had wrestled with and the momentous decisions they'd made right in that very room. And here were ol' "Dutch" Reagan and me yacking about baseball re-creates and vintage microphones.

Well, I guess it was for the best. I'm not really that good at discussing trickle-down economics and foreign policy.

In the blink of the eye, it was over. "It was a pleasure meeting you, Shotgun!" the President said.

It was time for me to make my exit. "It was an honor meeting you, Mr. President."

Duncan and I left the Oval Office, walked down the hallway, turned in our visitor passes, and walked out the double doors. Outside, KFMB news director Cliff Albert had set up two reporters from the Washington press to interview me on what had happened inside with President Reagan.

After the interview, Duncan and I got back into his beater car with the rope around the passenger side door and left the White House grounds. As we drove, we saw my brother Bob outside the White House waiting for me.

Duncan invited Bob to get in the car and said, "We're going to the Capitol building!" He'd had a long day, but the congressman still found the time to give my brother Bob and I a tour through the Capitol building and statuary hall. It's a day I will never, ever forget.

A few weeks later, my signed picture with the President arrived, but there was a problem. It just said, "To Tom Kelly." There was no "Shotgun." Making matters worse, I learned Mr. Reagan's signature was really a stamp they used so he wouldn't have to sign so many pictures.

I really wanted "Shotgun" in the dedication and I *really, really* wanted the president's actual signature. Luckily, Michael Reagan, the president's oldest son, was in San Diego doing a talk show on KSDO and we had become friendly. The package the White House sent me included two copies of the picture without a signature.

I contacted Michael, asking if the next time he visited his dad at the western White House in Santa Barbara, he could bring the picture with him and ask him to sign it. Michael said, "No problem."

Official White House photo

President Ronald Reagan and Shotgun Tom in the Oval Office at the White House.

Thanks to Michael, a few weeks later I had the picture. Now the dedication read, "To Shotgun Tom Kelly with very best wishes," and the signature was the real deal! I'm very grateful to Michael for that huge favor. That picture is one of my most prized possessions.

Sobriety For Me

This is going to be a tough chapter for me. I wasn't going to write it at all, but then I got to thinking that it might help someone who's in the same trouble I was in. If it will help even one person, I think it's worth it.

Sadly, my dad was a binge drinker. He'd be sober for long periods of time and then go on a bender, usually during the holidays and especially at Christmas. Many times, during my dad's "darker days", I would go and stay with my Aunt Ida and Uncle Roy. I was always confused because my dad was generally quite happy and personable. So, when he had these bouts of depression, I had a difficult time understanding why I was being shipped off to my aunt's house.

Luckily for me their son, Mike, who was the youngest of their seven children, was the same age as me. It took the sting out of having to leave home because we always had a great time hanging out together. In fact, although we would see each other over the holidays, a few years ago we also began having breakfast on a weekly basis. It began with just Mike and myself. Soon his nephew and my cousin, Billy, joined us along with several other friends, including Joe De La Cruz, Bill Calhoun, the owner of a mobile music company, and "Crazy" Dave Smith. Our breakfast club meets Wednesdays at Janet's Cafe. It's always a great time, as our boisterous group invades the restaurant, bringing lots of fun and laughs to the other patrons.

I idolized my older brothers Greg and Bob. I never saw them drink, and I wanted to be like them. I told myself that when I grow up, I'm surely not going to drink like dad. Now we know, thanks to a lot of research, that children of substance abusers are more likely to become abusers themselves than the average person. But that information wasn't available back then. I was a sitting duck, and I didn't even know it.

As I grew into my teenage years, I had no desire to drink. I was more interested in being in my bedroom with my make-believe radio station and having fun. My friends would always be interested in having a party and making sure that their parents were out so they could raid the liquor cabinet and try drinking some of the hard liquor. They would say, "Oh, come on, Tom, take a sip, you'll like it." I took a sip and it tasted horrible. I hated it. So that reinforced my desire not to drink. Ever.

My friend, Tom Brown, lived across the street. His dad always kept a beer keg in the garage icebox. When he wasn't home, we would always put our mouths under the spout and take a mouthful of beer. Again, the other kids loved it and laughed, but I failed to see the humor in it. I didn't like the taste of beer, either. I guess I was pretty much of a square when I was a kid. My friends were into cars and girls and I was into radio and radio towers.

I wasn't a big fan of marijuana, either. In 1967, when I was 17 or 18, I was working at KPRI FM with my friend Jim Chandler playing middle-of-the-road music.

Larry Shushan, the owner and general manager, decided that he wanted to try underground album rock radio from midnight to 6 in the morning to see if it would be a better way to get more listeners and advertisers.

The format caught on and Larry began expanding it to other day parts. He started hiring hippie-type DJs with weird names like O.B. Jetty, Achmad the Revolving and Gabriel Wisdom. The writing was on the wall. Jim and I saw we were going to be fired, and these guys would be taking over.

We heard through the grapevine that some of them might be smoking marijuana in the studio, which outraged Jim and I. That gave me a great idea … or so I thought. We would call the San Diego police and get the place raided. We actually did call the cops and Jim and I waited and waited for the police to come, but they never showed up. I'm glad they didn't.

Looking back, I wouldn't have wanted to get those guys in trouble for doing the same things I would be doing just a few years later, and doing a lot. KPRI FM soon went all hippie all the time. Jim and I were out. Jim changed his name from Chandler to Duncan and got a job at KSON, which had a country format. Jim stayed in the country-western radio business pretty much the rest of his career. I headed north to the Ogden school to get my "ticket."

My drinking days started in August 1970. I was working in Ventura/Oxnard and on August 8, 1970, I was going to turn 21. My buddy and fellow jock Dave Conley wanted to take me out for my 21st birthday and get me drunk for the first time. I told Dave I hated the taste of booze and didn't drink. He said he had just the drink for me, a Singapore Sling, mostly fruit, juice, and very little booze, but it does the trick.

Don McCulloch, a fellow KPRI FM alumnus, drove up from San Diego to get in on the fun. And oh, what fun we had! I must have downed five or six Singapore Slings.

I was drunk for the first time, feeling warm and fuzzy and very happy. Don took me home to my apartment and I crawled into bed and went to sleep. I got up the next morning thinking I was going to have a hangover, but I didn't. I felt fine. Maybe this stuff wasn't so bad after all.

Then Dave said I needed to expand my consciousness and start smoking marijuana. He said it opens up the mind and you can listen to music much better.

So I started smoking weed on a regular basis and fell in love with it. It made me feel relaxed. I wasn't out of control, which sometimes happened with booze. Music sounded so much better. I swore I could hear things you don't hear when you're straight.

In Bakersfield, Dave and I moved in together and started smoking lots of marijuana, and I even started drinking some natural carbonation beer.

Every Christmas, a record promoter named Rich Paladino would give Dave and me a gallon jug of red wine from Martoni's, the legendary hangout for people in the radio and record business in Hollywood. Once, I drank a whole jug all by myself.

Then I remembered my dad's Christmas drinking. Was I following in his footsteps? Like father, like son? No, I decided. My dad got moody and angry. I just got happy. So this was different. Or so I told myself.

Poor Dave Conley was a true alcoholic. He always said that he had to have a morning beer just to get his day started. In those days, booze wasn't that important to me, but I sure loved smoking marijuana. I felt mellow and dreamy. I didn't want to be an alcoholic like my dad and Dave, so I stuck to smoking marijuana, which was just fine for me.

If I'd left it like that, I might have been OK. The booze wasn't a problem and although I really liked my weed, I wasn't actually "addicted."

But, as a wise man once said: "Everybody's got a Jones, it's just that some folks are lucky enough to live their entire lives never finding out what theirs is."

I found out mine in 1971.

I was working for Buzz Bennett at KCBQ in San Diego. One day, while I was on the air, Buzz walked in the control room and said that he had a gift for me. He opened up a little vial of cocaine, and I tried it. It was love at first snort.

At first I was struck by the odor. It smelled like medicine in my nostrils. Then, a few minutes later, it kicked in. Wow! Suddenly my senses brightened, and I felt filled with boundless energy and confidence.

What can I say? The stuff made me feel really, really good. I loved the way it made me feel, and after that I wanted more!

For years, they told us that marijuana leads to harder drugs. Was it true? I guess my good experiences with weed left me more prone to experiment with other stuff and I can't really blame Buzz. There was so much coke around in those days that I'm sure I would have tried it sooner or later. And once I'd tried it – Katie, bar the door!

I continued my cocaine use with other folks. In those days, it was standard at a party for a couple of people to step into the bathroom and start lining up cocaine to snort. It was no big deal. Everybody was doing it.

The way you bought cocaine then was in a little paper wrapper that held three and a half grams. That was called an eight ball; one-eighth of an ounce is three and a half grams. You could do a half a gram by yourself and sell the other three grams and get back the $300 you'd spent on the eight ball.

Well, I loved cocaine so much that I did it the opposite way. I snorted the three grams and shared the half with my friends. My logic obviously wasn't working out.

Nor were my finances.

As for finding friends with whom to snort cocaine? It wasn't hard. All of them were doing it. It was just the thing to do, smoking marijuana and doing cocaine. That way you could adjust your buzz.

If you got too high on marijuana, you snorted cocaine. It brightened you up and brought you down to where you wanted to be.

I remember one time at a rock concert I was up in a private box at the stadium. There was even a nice private bathroom. Two other guys and I went into the bathroom. I had the blow. I laid out some lines.

The two were professional football players. I said to them, "You guys are so physically fit. Are you ever going to quit this?"

They stopped and thought about it, then looked at me and said, "NO!!" Then they started snorting my lines.

For me, one of the enjoyments about doing cocaine was sharing it with others. But as I got more hooked, I wasn't sharing it anymore. I was doing it all by myself.

That should have been a red flag. I found myself in unsavory situations with some very questionable people. People I would never have spent any time with normally, but if they had the coke, they were my new "friends."

Another red flag for me occurred the time my friend, who we'll call "Dave," said he was in town and had some cocaine he wanted to do with me. I told him I had to stay at the TV station, but my additional work would only take me two hours. "Can I meet you in two hours?" I asked.

"OK, I'll wait for you."

Two hours later, I called Dave from a phone booth. I couldn't get him to answer the phone. I called and called and called. By now, I stood in that phone booth, pissed. I wanted that cocaine!!

He didn't pick up. I started slamming the receiver against the payphone. The plastic receiver fell to pieces at my feet. I was a madman!

To this day, I can't believe my behavior. I'm so ashamed. But I decided to tell this story to illustrate how drugs can turn an easygoing, fun-loving person into a monster.

I drank, smoked grass and did cocaine for at least 15 years. They say before you can get clean, you have to hit bottom.

Hitting bottom can be different things for different people. Sadly, for some, like my old friend Dave Conley who bought me my first legal drink and who died of liver failure after years of heavy drinking, hitting bottom is death.

My bottom happened at a wedding. After the ceremony, we went to the hotel suite and one guy had a whole bag of cocaine. I couldn't believe how big it was. I stayed there all night long and didn't get home until 9 a.m. Sunday … just in time to go to Mass.

Linda asked where I'd been. "I was at the wedding."

"The wedding was over with at 8 p.m. last night!"

"Well, I went to the after party," I replied.

Then I told her the story about the guy with all that cocaine, and she couldn't believe it. She said, "You've got to do something about this habit. You need to quit."

Then she reminded me that we were in the process of adopting a child. That hit me like a brick.

I *had* to stop drinking and using!

So the next day, Monday, I went over to Kirby Winn's barbershop. I knew that he had been in a 12-step program and it had really worked for him. I told him I wanted to quit drinking. I told him I wanted to quit snorting cocaine and smoking marijuana. I wanted to quit it all!

He suggested I come to a meeting at the McDonald's Center up in La Jolla – a suburb of San Diego – on Wednesday night. It's a treatment center where people go and stay for 30 days to stop their addiction to pills, alcohol, marijuana or cocaine. It's also the location for 12-step group meetings.

That was my very first meeting. I shared, and really got into the program. I was there every Wednesday night. I went to other meetings, too, in the park and at various church halls. We had so many great speakers. Bobby Orman, Will Wainess, Dr. John Faessel, Bob Palmer and my sponsor, Kirby Winn.

On Christmas Eve 1984, the day Linda and I also welcomed our son Nick into our family, I became clean and sober. A new son and sobriety. Two of the best things that have ever happened to me.

Four weeks later, with only 29 days of sobriety under my belt, I did a very foolhardy thing. I went up to Hollywood to see an old friend, the legendary DJ Wolfman Jack, immortalized in the movie *American Graffiti* and the song "Clap for the Wolfman" by the Guess Who. I took my friend John Fewel with me, and I'm sure glad I did.

As we walked into Wolf's studio at Hollywood and Vine, Wolf was throwing darts at a target attached to the back of the studio door. He thought I was alone, so after I came in, Wolf threw another dart and almost hit John. He felt it whistle by about three inches from his nose!

The Wolf apologized profusely.

Once seated at the table in the Wolf's studio, he looked at me and asked, "Where is your offering?"

That puzzled me. "What do you mean by an offering?" I asked.

The Wolf paused for a moment and stared at me. He then explained, "It's customary that whenever someone is granted an audience with the Wolfman, that someone is to present Wolfman with an offering.

"I'm sorry," I replied, "But I don't have any cocaine or anything like that."

The Wolf went on to explain that he didn't mean cocaine, he meant marijuana and the Wolf felt that weed was not a drug.

Then John spoke up and told Wolfman that he had some great home-grown in Shotgun's car. Wolfman declined and reached into his coat pocket and pulled out an ancient looking rolled up leather pouch.

As we sat and talked, the Wolf pulled out a big beautifully manicured marijuana bud and put it on the table in front of me. I could smell the resin off the bud. Then Wolfman pulled out an already rolled joint and said, “Well, boys, I guess we’re just gonna have to smoke some of mine.”

Now, remember, I’m only 29 days sober and I was going to get my 30-day token the next day at the McDonald’s Treatment Center in La Jolla.

The Wolfman lit up the joint, took a hit and passed it to me and I looked at it and started thinking *I only have 29 days, I could smoke this joint with the Wolfman and start all over again.*

But then, God bless him, John said, “Tom, tell the Wolfman why you’re not going to smoke that joint.”

I took a deep breath. “Wolf, I can’t smoke with you. I’m 29 days clean. I don’t snort cocaine, use marijuana or drink anymore.”

He smiled and tilted his head and he said, “Oh, that’s beautiful, man!” Then he winked and said, “You’re not gonna *preach* to me, are you?” Wolf and John smoked the joint there in front of me.

Later, as we drove back down to San Diego, John said, “I’m really impressed with this 12-step thing. I never would have believed you’d turn down a chance to smoke weed with Wolfman Jack!”

Photo from Irwin Family Archives

Shotgun Tom with Wolfman Jack.

I found it hard to believe, too, but that's exactly what I did.

Of course I hadn't partaken, but I was in the same room where it happened. So, the next day I called Kirby, now my sponsor. He was basically the overseer of my sobriety and the person with whom I checked in on all matters regarding the program.

"Kirby, I was in a room where they smoked marijuana yesterday," I said. "Do you think I relapsed?"

"Did you actually take the marijuana in your lips?" He asked.

"No, I didn't." He said that I was fine and that I'd be able to get my 30-day token on that night. Linda and all my friends were there. I told my story and I got my token, which felt like quite an accomplishment for myself.

An interesting postscript to the Wolfman story is that John managed to get the roach clip and the roach from his smoke session with the Wolfman.

He had them embedded in a block of clear lucite made in the shape of a pen and pencil holder. There's a picture of John and the Wolfman and the inscription, "What is left of the joint I smoked with Wolfman Jack."

Nice piece of memorabilia!

Once at the McDonald's Center Desi Arnaz, living in Del Mar at the time, put in an appearance. I was so stoked!

I wanted to meet him because I was a huge admirer of this bandleader, musician, singer, actor and producer, the man who co-founded Desilu Studios with his then-wife Lucille Ball when they produced and starred in their legendary sitcom "I Love Lucy."

Thanks to its revolutionary 3-film camera technique at a time when no one thought these shows would ever be aired again, the superior picture quality meant that "I Love Lucy" aired in reruns for decades and is still available today on streaming services and DVD.

Did I mention I'm a big fan? But before I could approach him, I was invited to the podium to share my sobriety story. I got up and got carried away. Speaking of the depths of my addiction, I said "Man, I used to get really f***ed up. I was so f***ed up all the time!"

After my talk, I sauntered over to Mr. Arnaz and introduced

myself. “Hi, I’m Shotgun Tom Kelly.”

He glared at me and said, “I know who you are! You are the host of a local television show for children. YOU GOT A DIRTY MOUTH! You should NOT talk the way you just did tonight in public!”

Wow! I did not expect that! Ricky Ricardo was chewing out my ass! But I have to admit he was right. I’ve since cleaned up my 12-step talks.

Another celebrity I met during my “getting sober days” was actor Danny Trejo. I was asked to speak at a treatment center in Malibu and found out that Danny Trejo was also a guest speaker. After our day at the center, we became fast friends and attended a few 12-step meetings together.

Photo from Irwin Family Archives

Shotgun Tom with Danny Trejo.

Danny, along with being a successful actor, also owns Trejo Tacos, a chain of Los Angeles taco shops. I'm here to tell you his tacos are not only healthy, but absolutely delicious. He offers many varieties of tacos, including vegan.

For the past several years I've been in the Hollywood Christmas Parade, riding in Gary Goltz's "Broderick Crawford" Highway Patrol car.

One year Danny was the grand marshal of the parade. It was great being on the red carpet together.

Take it from me, if you're in the L.A. area make sure to visit Trejo Tacos. You will become an instant fan.

Photos from Irwin Family Archives

Shotgun Tom waving to fans in the vintage Highway Patrol car in the Hollywood Christmas Parade.

I want to close this chapter by saying if you, or someone you know, is in the grip of addiction, it doesn't have to be that way. There's plenty of help out there these days. Find a good program and work it. You'll meet some wonderful people who are there to lend a hand without judging you.

Odds are good, no matter how bad your story is, they've been there, too. Some will have even sadder tales to tell than you.

The bottom line is you'll end up getting and staying sober together and helping others do the same. And I've got to tell you, helping others is just about the best high I've ever experienced.

If I can do it, you can do it! **Check this out: as of December 24, 2024, I'll be 40 years Clean and Sober!**

See Shotgun Tom on KFMB CBS 8 TV talking about Wolfman Jack following the legendary DJ's death in 1995.

The Hands Of Fate

It was 1991 and here I was, sober and ready to take on the world. But the world just wasn't cooperating.

For the first time since I was a teenager, I couldn't find a full-time radio job. The weekend gig at KFMB AM, with the Corvette Diner broadcast, was a lot of fun, but the part-time gig certainly didn't pay enough to support the family.

But try as I might, I just wasn't able to make anything happen. Part of it was wanting to stay in San Diego. If I'd been willing to pick up stakes and move somewhere else, it might have been a different story.

We had a house in a nice neighborhood, the kids were in great schools, and Linda and I loved the San Diego lifestyle. But the money was running out fast and I began to wonder if we were going to lose the house.

Still, sometimes, if you're lucky, fate reaches out and lends a hand just when you need it the most. That's what happened to me back then … and I'll never forget it. Aside from the weekend radio show, the only steady income I had at the time was doing radio and TV commercials for a chain of consumer electronics stores called Mad Jack's.

They had seven locations in San Diego. The car stereo business was booming in those days. It seemed like back then everybody was busy putting after-market stereo systems into their cars and trucks, and Mad Jack's was doing a ton of sales and installation. I was happy to have the gig, but even with Linda's radio traffic salary, it was barely enough to pay the mortgage.

One day, when I stopped by the office of Bruce Bart, Mad Jack's president, he introduced me to David Black, the executive vice president of Alpine Electronics of America, a company that built high-end car audio and security systems. Dave and I hit it off and he asked me to come up to the Alpine Electronics headquarters in Torrance, California to talk about an idea he had for a car audio competition. He called it Car Audio Nationals, and he wanted to hire me to be his spokesman and help promote it.

Dave said he wanted me to become totally immersed in their products, and he had his assistant VP of tech services, Rich Coe, outfit my van with an amazing custom 2000W audio system with security and mobile phone.

To this day, friends talk about how I used to demonstrate the system for them and how they've never forgotten the clarity of the sound they heard in my van. There were 26 speakers, four subwoofers in the back and a head unit with CD player in the dash, custom installed by Alpine Electronics. Dave also put in a complete Alpine security system.

What a way to get familiar with the products that I'm about ready to promote all over the country!

The idea was to go to a different city in the United States every weekend for 13 weeks and book myself on radio and television morning shows promoting Car Audio Nationals coming to their city that weekend.

The week before I came to each city, I called the prospective radio and TV stations and talked to the producers and got myself booked on different radio and TV shows.

My other job was being at the venue and when the news cameras came to cover the competition, I would be interviewed by the reporters, explaining what's going on with the competition and how it worked.

I'd always arrive two days before the event to make my radio and TV appearances promoting the show. Music radio stations understood the concept, but talk stations weren't that keen on promoting something that might lure their listeners away to music radio, so we had to use another approach.

Alpine Electronics had hired a reformed car thief named Don Bledsoe, who once worked as a repo man for General Motors, to be our spokesman on talk radio stations. He told amazing stories about breaking into cars to repossess them, and spoke about how listeners could protect their cars with an Alpine security system.

Don was always at the event with a demonstration on how fast he could break into a car and pointed out that if you had an Alpine security system, it would be a lot more difficult for him because of the alarm that would go off. He was a big hit at the shows.

Alpine Electronics also had a camera man on board. Frank Vilics, who worked as a free-lance camera man for major TV networks, joined us on our 13-week tour. Frank was always hurrying us along because we tended to lag in the morning.

Since we were required to arrive at many of the broadcast facilities as guests on their morning shows, we were awakened many times with Frank rapping on our hotel room doors.

Now I've been known to run late, but Don was even slower than I was. So, when Frank knocked on Don's door he'd chant over and over, "Let's go, Bledsoe!!" The three of us hit it off and enjoyed crossing the country together, introducing our audiences to Alpine car audio electronics.

I have very fond memories of my Car Audio National days. In fact, to this day whenever my family and I are leaving to go somewhere, you can hear us repeating Frank's little chant, "Let's go, Bledsoe!!" And even though Don and Frank have long since passed away, we have kept their memory alive.

We raised money from the entry fees. There were two categories to enter your car, regular customer or professional customer. The regular customers would be private individuals who had a hot stereo system they'd installed themselves.

The install was crucial. It had to look like it was part of the car.

Everything had to be ergonomically correct, and the sound pure. The judges placed a microphone inside the car with a test system to record the sound and detect any distortion.

The professional customers were people who owned car audio stores and wanted to compete with other stores. The event was free to the public and all proceeds went to The Muscular Dystrophy Association and Jerry's Kids.

It was a lot of fun for me to go from city to city and see a lot of my buddies working around the country in radio and TV and go on the air with them to promote the event. We were on many television morning talk shows like "Good Morning, Chicago," "Good Morning, Denver" and "Good Morning, Mobile, Alabama."

When I did the morning show in Mobile, the host wanted to know what I thought of the town. I suddenly remembered this dumb thing my buddy John Fewel used to call me: "Big Deal McNeil from Mobile." I don't know where he came up with it, but he hit me with it a bunch of times.

At that moment it popped into my head and I said to the host, "You know, I must tell you I've been treated marvelously here in Mobile. You folks have made me feel like Big Deal McNeil from Mobile!"

It was the dumbest thing, but luckily the host got a big kick out of it and laughed his ass off. I have no idea what the viewers thought.

At first doing the job was fun, but I soon began to appreciate how rough it is for entertainers who are on the road for months on end. The relentless grind of plane rides, hotels, crisscrossing multiple time zones, all the promotional appearances and the events every weekend really started to wear me down. Still, I was more than grateful for the work and the ability to start paying off some long overdue bills thanks to Dave Black and Alpine Electronics.

After the final city, the cars that had scored the highest were shipped to San Diego's Sea World to compete in the Car Audio Grand Nationals. Dave Black and Alpine Electronics hired a big television production truck with director and crew to record the event. A short time later, during the MDA Labor Day Telethon, Dave Black presented my old pal Jerry Lewis a big check from Car Audio Nations.

So it was a win-win for all concerned, and I got to keep my house. But looking back, there's no doubt in my mind that I could never have pulled it off had I still been drinking and using.

CHAPTER 18

Bay Area Boogie

In the early Eighties, I had the great opportunity to work at one of the most legendary AM radio stations in the country: The Big 610 KFRC AM in San Francisco.

Jerry Cagle, then program director, called and asked if I was available to work some vacation relief. I jumped at the chance and soon was on my way to working at one of my dream radio stations.

Lucky me! When I arrived, I felt at home because so many of my friends were employed at the station. Dave Sholin, Doctor Don Rose, Sue Hall, Harry Nelson, and Bobby Ocean were on-air personalities. The chief engineer, Phil Lerza, was a great friend and I'll always be grateful that, because I had a first-class FCC license, he included my name on the roster of engineers. Wow!

It was Phil's idea to build a mobile studio in

a motor home (Phil called it "the Sturgeon") to do remote broadcasts from various locations. It included everything that the KFRC in-house studios had. What a studio it was! I remember broadcasting from Union Square in front of the St. Francis Hotel. Thank you, Jerry Cagle, for giving me this once in a lifetime opportunity.

The Greatest Show On "Earth"

Donald Steele Revert, known professionally as "The Real" Don Steele, was born in Hollywood, California, and graduated from Hollywood High School. He pursued a career in radio and spent a number of years honing his skills at stations in the Midwest and Pacific Northwest until, in 1965, he got a chance to come back and broadcast in his hometown.

In 1965 Steele was chosen to host the afternoon drive slot, from 3 p.m. to 6 p.m., on 93 KHJ in Los Angeles. The station was flipping to a new, innovative format called Boss Radio, which as I noted earlier was the brainchild of radio programmer Bill Drake.

Boss Radio would change the sound of popular music radio in a big way. Echoes of its sound can still be heard on the radio dial today.

Basically, the format stripped away all the clutter bogging down the other stations at the time. DJ patter was cut back, but the jocks were directed to put total thought and concentration into what they'd do and say when they *did* speak. Less, somehow, became more, making the Boss Jocks, as they were known, actually more impactful than the long-winded DJs at other stations on the dial.

The number of commercials that the station aired was cut down, too, and the whole package became a high-energy mix of words and music that made other stations sound like they were standing still.

The format had proven astonishingly successful in Fresno and San Diego. KHJ would be the first test of the new format in a major market. The format debuted when Don Steele went on the air on KHJ at 3 p.m. on April 27, 1965. Los Angeles radio would never be the same.

Steele hit the air with an explosive energy. Talking at breakneck speed, sometimes so fast he became unintelligible, Steele spewed out a never-ending stream of very clever, very hip patter.

He was so over the top that he almost sounded unhinged at times, but those who knew or worked with him can attest that behind it all was a man of high intelligence and a strong work ethic.

He never gave less than one hundred percent. And what he did seemed custom-made for an afternoon audience dealing with the smog and car-clogged freeways of L.A., a city Steele described as "the concrete fun jungle."

There were many DJs over the years who worked at the various

Drake stations around the country who called themselves Boss Jocks, myself included. But the two Boss Jocks most revered and respected by the audience and their radio peers were Steele and KHJ morning DJ Robert W. Morgan.

With Robert getting them to work and school in the mornings and Steele steering them home in the afternoons, this one-two punch of radio talent helped keep KHJ at the top of the ratings for the better part of a decade.

Steele and Morgan both left KHJ in 1973 to join an FM station for which Bill Drake was consulting in Los Angeles. But FM still hadn't quite found its audience and the station was a failure in the ratings. For the next 10 years, both jocks bounced around the dial at various L.A. stations until, in 1992, they were reunited on KRTH 101, KHJ's older sister FM station.

By this time FM radio had come into its own and K-Earth (KRTH) was playing the hits of the Sixties and Seventies. With Morgan in the mornings and Steele in the afternoons, playing the same music they'd played in their heyday at KHJ, the old magic was reborn.

Steele, Morgan and KRTH 101 were back on top! Steele would receive a star on the Hollywood Walk of Fame in 1995.

Meanwhile, 120 miles to the south in San Diego, I was paying the bills with a number of hustles. After 12 years, my KUSI TV kids show was canceled so they could run an afternoon news block. This freed me up to become the voice of NBC 7/39, doing news intros and promos.

At the same time, I was also hosting a cigar show on KSDO AM news-talk radio. The show aired on Sunday afternoons for one hour. The radio station didn't pay me any money, but they did give me four commercial slots to sell to cigar stores in the San Diego area.

I sold to three cigar stores: Liberty Tobacco, The Tinderbox and Smitty's Cigars in Vista. I charged each of them $500 per show. So I was making $1,500 for that one-hour show every week.

The show originated from a restaurant called Trophy's, which had an adjacent cigar lounge. They called it the Club Fumar. I put up a stage like the one on the "Tonight Show" and booked local guests on the show. They included part-owner of the San Diego Chargers George Pernicano, veteran news anchor Hal Clement, former San Diego Mayor Roger Hedgecock, KUSI Sports anchor Rod Luck, and various friends of mine who owned the cigar stores.

I knew nothing about cigars, but luckily John Fewel knew everything about them, and he was my sidekick. Another old friend, Tony Pepper, produced the show, which we did live. Quite frankly, it was a lot of fun!

With my TV voiceover business and the radio show I was doing pretty well and that might have been all she wrote for me. Then something happened that changed my life and career in a big way.

On August 5, 1997, The Real Don Steele succumbed to lung cancer at age 61. Hearing the news in San Diego, I mourned the loss of one of my true radio heroes.

I was devastated. I loved listening to him on KRTH and now he was gone.

I was talking to my friend Riley Cardwell. Nobody could replace Don Steele, but the show had to go on. "Who do you think is going to replace him?" I asked.

Without taking so much as a breath Riley said, "You are."

"You've got to be kidding!" I replied.

"No, I'm not kidding," Riley said. "You're the only one who can do it. There is nobody else."

I didn't believe it, of course, only Riley was right.

A week later, the phone rang at our house and Linda answered. It was a call from the union, AFTRA-San Diego. They said they'd received a call from KRTH Radio in Los Angeles and they wanted to get in touch with me. AFTRA wanted to make sure it was all right for them to give out our phone number. Of course, Linda said, "YES!"

Honestly, we thought that maybe they wanted to hire me to do promos. It never occurred to us that they were actually interested in hiring me as The Real Don Steele's successor.

A few days later, K-Earth program director Mike Phillips called. He asked if I would come up and talk with him. I said I could, of course. He then asked me for an air check of one of my K-Best radio shows.

Uh-oh. *Something* was up! I had *that* feeling....

I went over to KSDO, where Tony Pepper was production director, and asked him to help me email this tape from K-Best up to KRTH. I told him that Mike Phillips and KRTH general manager Pat Duffy wanted to hear it.

Tony dropped everything he was doing and proceeded to digitize my air check and email it.

It was a Tuesday afternoon when I first walked into the KRTH 101 studios, then at the corner of Venice and Fairfax in Los Angeles. Mike Phillips' assistant, Chrissy Hamilton, met me in the lobby and walked me down the hall to Pat Duffy's office, where Pat and Mike Phillips were waiting for me.

They offered me a seat and pleasantries were exchanged. Then Mike said, "We want you to succeed The Real Don Steele – will you do it?"

Without hesitation I said, "Yes!"

"Great! Now it's my turn," Pat said. "What's going to make you happy?"

"What do you mean?" I asked.

"How much money do you want?"

The question had taken me by surprise because I thought the meeting was merely an interview. I found out later that I was actually their first choice.

Buying some time, I told them I'd need to speak with Linda and asked to use a phone. Instead, I called my attorney, Bob

Teaff, in La Jolla and told him what had just happened. "How much should I ask for?"

Bob named a figure and I almost dropped the phone.

"Bob, I can't ask for that kind of money! It's only a three-hour show weekdays in afternoon drive. If I demand that kind of money, they'll laugh me out of the building!"

"Don't demand it," Bob replied. "Just politely ask for it."

My knees were a-knockin', but I took a deep breath, went in there and asked for the amount of money that Bob suggested. "Is that all you want?" Pat replied.

"Yes."

"Absolutely. You've got it! Plus, we'll build in incentives with the ratings, and you can make more money."

Done deal!

I guess it helped that Dan Mason, president of Infinity Broadcasting, KRTH's owners at the time, was a fan of mine. I'd met him in Kansas City along with his PD, Chris Bailey, when I was with KCBQ and Dan was doing middays at KBEQ.

He'd said at the time that he was thrilled to meet me and that he used to call in on the listen line from Kansas City to hear my show on KCBQ.

Little did I know that years later I would be working for him at KRTH 101 and Infinity Broadcasting. When

Infinity sold CBS Radio, Dan Mason then became president of CBS Radio.

My first day at K-Earth was September 18, 1997. I signed on promptly at 3 p.m. with "Shotgun" by Junior Walker and the All Stars.

I did my intro over the record, and I remember the chief engineer Lynn Duke opening the studio door and saying "Wow! That was great! Welcome to K-Earth 101!"

I had an engineer who handled the equipment. We called him Elvis, but his real name was Mike Burkholder. He was so helpful.

And I was understandably very nervous about sitting in the same chair that my hero, The Real Don Steele, had once sat in.

After I'd been there a week, my friend and morning man, the legendary Robert W. Morgan, called in on the hot line. "Weren't you going to call me?" he asked.

"Yes, I was going to call you," I said, "but I wanted to make sure I felt that I had my act together first."

Robert chuckled and said, "Welcome to K-Earth 101!" That was really great, coming from him.

The staff lineup at KRTH consisted of Robert W. Morgan in the morning, Brian Beirne, "Mr. Rock 'n' Roll," from 9 a.m. to noon, Johnny Hayes from noon to 3 p.m., and yours truly from 3 to 6 p.m. Jay Coffey handled evenings and Bill Stevens took listeners through the night. On the weekends we had

Steve Jay, Jim Carson, Dave Randall and Chaz Kelly.

Another one of my radio heroes was the weekend jock, Steve Jay. I wanted to meet him because I grew up listening to him when he worked at KGB in San Diego. Steve was so gracious when I told him about being a former listener.

After KGB, Steve went up to San Francisco to work for Drake station KFRC and changed his name to Jay Stevens. I really admired his work. Over the years he just got better and better. And now here we were working at the same station.

Mike Phillips told me a truly amazing story. He said that after he'd attended Don Steele's memorial, he had gone back to the station, knelt down by his desk and said a prayer. "God," he prayed. "Please help me find the right guy to succeed The Real Don Steele."

Mike said he'd heard a whisper, "Call Shotgun Tom."

That proved to me that the reason I was working at KRTH was a spiritual one.

Had my many years living clean and sober been rewarded? Had God, perhaps, decided to take a hand?

I'll never know, but I'll always be so grateful that Mike heard and responded to that whisper.

Mike said that he wanted to recut my jingle, so he called Johnny Mann and scheduled some session time at a big recording studio called The Bakery. Don Shelton and Melissa McKay were Johnny Mann's singers and friends of mine.

Mike Phillips and Jay Coffey were in the studio, with Mike telling Johnny what he wanted the singers to sing. The jingle came out great, and all these years later I still use it on SiriusXM Sixties Gold Channel 73.

Dave Sholin was running the radio tip sheet, *The Gavin Report*, and he wanted to introduce KRTH's new afternoon drive personality – me! – at the Gavin Convention in San Diego.

The convention was held at the Manchester Grand Hotel. We all had to enter the convention room though the kitchen so none of the radio people at the convention could see us in the lobby.

Joining me on the panel were the new San Diego morning team Jeff and Jer from Q106, Charlie Tuna of K-BIG, and Shaune Steele, The Real Don Steel's widow.

I remember saying to Shaune, "I'm not replacing The Real Don Steele, I'm succeeding him."

Both Linda and I were instantly taken with how warm and welcoming Shaune was to both of us. From that moment forward we all became very good friends, and Linda and I enjoyed her friendship ever since that magical day in 1997.

Unfortunately, Shaune fell ill in late 2023. We were devastated when she passed away that December 29th.

Helluva way to start a new year, huh?

Back at the convention, the audience was crammed with top

radio people like my old boss Buzz Bennett, Pat Martin, Art Vuolo and others.

What a rush!

I got to work with some real great pro's at KRTH. It was so good to be on the air there. The station's on-air audio chain was put together by engineers Bob Kanter and Lynn Duke.

The studios were gorgeous. The audio proved to be the best I have ever worked with in my long career. It could turn a whisper into a roar. The equipment was state of the art and worked flawlessly. It was the radio big time and the ol' Shotgun was having a ball!

Watch the Johnny Mann Singers record the Shotgun Tom jingle.

L.A. Daze

In 1997, when I was first hired at KRTH and getting ready to relocate from San Diego to Los Angeles, Linda and I decided that we'd keep our house in San Diego. She'd continue to live there and I'd come home on weekends. Since I got off the air on Friday evening and didn't have to be back until midday on Mondays, that would give me two full days a week in San Diego with Linda. Now the question was, where would I live during my five days in Los Angeles?

Everybody I asked had a different opinion about where I should live. Legendary jazz radio personality Chuck Niles lived in Marina Del Rey and suggested his community. A lot of others recommended one of the many neighborhoods in the San Fernando Valley – or, as it's normally referred to by Angelenos, "The Valley."

My friend Tony Pepper, who had lived in Los Angeles for a few years, said, "You don't want to live someplace people refer to as The F'n Valley!"

He suggested I check out Park La Brea. He believed it would be perfect for me because of its proximity to the KRTH studios, and cool old-school vibe. Park La Brea is one of those large self-contained corporate apartment communities originally built in the Forties with eighteen 12-floor towers surrounded by about 30 garden-style apartment clusters, with a total of over 4,000 units. Not much has changed since these places were built. They had extra-large steel framed windows you had to open with a crank, and only some of the appliances had been upgraded to 1970-ish technology.

There was no air conditioning, and only those old-style steel piped heaters that brought the heat up from some furnace in the basement, which didn't work very well. It was kind of hot in the summer, and a little cold in the winter. But still a very cool place to live.

Park La Brea is located in the middle of all the action. It stands across the street from the Farmers Market, what was then CBS Television City, The Grove, and just a short walk to the world-famous La Brea Tarpits. The Miracle Mile on Wilshire Boulevard is close by, and so were a lot of my soon-to-be favorites, like Canter's Deli.

Tony advised me to not get one of the garden units that faced any of the busy streets that bordered the complex. He suggested I look at one of the tower apartments, as that would be in a safer spot, and some of the units have amazing views of Hollywood or downtown.

I did as he suggested, immediately falling in love with the place. I spent the next 20 years on the 12th floor of Tower 47 with a view of the Hollywood sign on Mount Lee and the radio towers on Mount Wilson.

The residents at Park LaBrea are a very close-knit group, many of them having lived there for decades. I was told, "You move into Park LaBrea, you leave in a body bag." Over the months and years, I became good friends with all of my neighbors on my floor and many others throughout the neighborhood.

A lot of celebrities live (or have lived) at Park La Brea. Jay Ward, who created the characters Rocky and Bullwinkle, had lived and sketched those characters in my building.

Alex Haley, the author of *Roots*, lived in my unit before I moved into it, and it wasn't uncommon to get in the elevator with someone famous like actor Laurence Fishburne or musician Terry Kirkman from The Association.

I adapted to living in Los Angeles better than I could have imagined. Of course, there was the thrill of working in the No. 2 radio market in the United States at a legendary radio station, but there was also the magic of living so close to Hollywood.

My family loved visiting me at Park La Brea and walking across the street to the Farmer's Market. We enjoyed breakfast at Du-Par's Restaurant, where you'll find the best pancakes ever made!

If you are ever in Los Angeles, you definitely have got to try them. They are so good on their own that butter and syrup are not required!

And, of course, there's Canter's Deli on Fairfax, the very

restaurant where my family and I had one of our first Los Angeles meals. I began frequenting Canter's and felt at home with the staff. I struck up a friendship with the Canter family members, Gary, Jackie and Marc.

I always looked forward to chatting with them whenever I dropped in after my shift at KRTH. Many times I was accompanied by some of my friends, including Norm Jacobovitz, Chuck McCann (movie TV and commercial actor), the legendary comedy genius Stan Freberg, Los Angeles city council member Tom LaBonge, Gary Goltz, radio personality Tom Leykis, and former record promotors Steve Resnick and Don Whittemore.

To this day whenever I'm in Los Angeles, a trip to Canter's is always on my agenda.

One of my neighbors, who had lived there since the early Sixties, was known as "The Countess," a chain-smoking, wealthy elderly lady who claimed to be a real Countess from Sweden. Her apartment was twice the size of mine, and was filled with original art, signed photos, collectables, and memorabilia from celebrities and political leaders from all corners of the world.

She owned several hand-woven rugs from the Middle East worth over $20,000 each and on which she would drop cigarette ash and bacon grease. There was a signed baseball from Mickey Mantle casually placed on an end table, a signed photo from JFK on one of her nightstands, and so much more.

Among the artwork hanging on her walls was a piece she claimed was painted by Rembrandt's understudy and was pre-pledged to the Getty Museum upon her passing.

The Countess was also owner of a one-of-a-kind classic Mercedes Benz. It was parked, uncovered, down in one of the parking garages, side by side with all the run-of-the-mill Camrys and SUVs.

I'm not much of a car guy, but it was from the Fifties or Sixties, with the gull-winged doors that opened vertically. She said there were only a few of that model made and it was a gift from someone at Mercedes Benz. It was rare and worth a lot.

I've never seen another one like it, ever.

Fast-forward a few years to May 1999. Tony Pepper got a gig at a post-production studio in Santa Monica.

He needed a place to stay for a few months while he and his wife found a home of their own, so he temporarily moved into my extra bedroom. Tony had more of a 9-to-6 schedule, while I was on KRTH from 4 to 7 p.m.

We would meet back at the apartment after work, head out for dinner, then return to the apartment to smoke a cigar and watch another San Diego media refugee, Harold Greene, on the 11 p.m. news. We would talk loudly, laugh loudly, and cuss loudly, with the TV turned up way too loud.

Later that summer, the Countess let me know her Mercedes was at Simonson Mercedes Benz in Santa Monica. They had given her car a complete detail and had it looking like brand new again, and it was on display in the showroom for everyone to see. She really wanted Tony and me to go to the dealership to see it.

After dinner one night, halfway through our cigars with the 11 p.m. news turned up too loud, I mentioned going to see her car. Between puffs and not missing a beat, Tony unloaded a locker room-type response with words that begin with F, S, and C, that would have made former Dodger manager Tommy Lasorda take a step back.

I said, "Oh, come on, Tony let's make the Countess happy!" Tony offered up another profanity-filled response. I shouted, "Don't be an asshole!!"

Tony kept screaming, "You can go, but I'm NOT going!!" with a few more words beginning with the letter F. We were really, really loud.

A few minutes later, there was a knock at the door. It was after 11:30 p.m., on a warm summer night. Our shorts were on, our shirts were off. Who could be at the door at this hour? I got up with my "Shotgun Tom" hat on, shirtless and cigar in hand, and answered the door. All Tony could see from his vantage point across the room was my bare back, a cloud of cigar smoke, and me talking to someone saying, "No, no, that's cool."

"No, no, no, we're good. I understand. Yes, yes, no, no, no."

I went back and sat down in my chair with what must have been a stunned look on my face. Tony asked me who was at the door. I remember just sitting there for a few moments quietly staring at the TV. Tony asked, "Was it the Countess? Was it Charlie Band and his girlfriend Robin Sydney from next door? Are we making too much noise in here?"

I leaned over and whispered in Tony's direction, "No, it wasn't the Countess. It was my neighbor from downstairs. I think he's had a few cocktails, and he can hear us up here laughing and cussing, and he thinks we're up here having crazy sex!"

The neighbor had said, "I'm gay, and I know you guys are gay, too.

I said, "No, no, no."

"That's OK, but when you guys have sex up here, you are loud!" He said. "It's OK with me, but I've got my mom and dad visiting. If you guys can just hold it down for the rest of this week and when they leave you two can be as loud as you want. I like listening to you guys up there."

Now, Tony was the one with the stunned look on his face. A few puffs later, Tony asks, "Do you know him?"

I had never met him, I didn't know who he was.

The next day I got home from the station and found an envelope underneath my door. Inside was a hand-written note: "Please forgive me for knocking on your door so late last night. My parents leave this Sunday; after that you and your friend can make as much noise as you want. I'm totally good with it. And let's make a date for both of you guys to come down to my place for a few drinks, and let's get better acquainted!"

We never took him up on his invitation, but it did make for

some interesting trips in the elevator whenever "Bill" and I happened to share it all the way up to the 12th floor.

There is one more rather amusing story about the Countess. One morning, as I was going to run a few errands, the Countess caught me leaving my apartment and asked if I could take some of her letters to the post office. Seems like this errand should have been a rather run-of-the-mill chore. Well, not so. I was fairly well known at the neighborhood "Grove" post office and so was the Countess. So, when it was my turn, I handed the clerk the letters and as an afterthought said, "Oh by the way, the Countess sends her regards. The clerk smiled, acknowledged this, and said that she sends back her regards as well.

Later on, as I was leaving for my air shift, the Countess caught me a second time and asked if I fulfilled her errand. I replied that indeed I had, and not only did I take the letters into the post office, but I handed them directly to the clerk and even gave her "your kind regards."

Thinking that the Countess would give me an attaboy, she turned every shade of purple and said, "You must never give my regards to anyone without my permission." And with that she turned and stormed back into her apartment and slammed the door.

I was so taken aback with the absurdity of the scenario that I just shook my head and went on my way to KRTH.

A few days later I had to mail a package and sought out the same postal clerk. After accepting the package from me she said, "Oh by the way, the Countess came over the other day and actually took back her regards that you unofficially gave to me."

We looked at each other and burst out laughing.

Thinking back, this sounds too ridiculous to be true, but it actually happened. By the way, it took weeks before the Countess even acknowledged my existence. Naturally, the turning point, came when she needed another favor.

She was definitely one of a kind.

I spent nearly 20 years at KRTH 101 and it was quite an experience. I remember my first day signing on. I couldn't believe I was in the same studio The Real Don Steele had broadcast from. I settled in and gradually got to know some of my co-workers.

One of the guys I worked with was Keith Smith, a world-class editor, who produced all the promos for the station. Another guy I met was Brandon Castillo, who was one of Robert W. Morgan's producers. He befriended me and always seemed to know what was going on at the station. He always kept me updated, for which I was very grateful.

As I mentioned, Robert W. Morgan and I were friends before I came to Los Angeles. The thing was it was "Robert," NOT "Bob." One time he called me, and Linda answered the phone. Robert asked if I was home and Linda said I wasn't, but that I'd be back soon. "Please tell him that Robert called," said Robert.

To which Linda replied, "OK, Bob."

The next thing she heard was Robert screaming, "NO BOB LIVES HERE!!!" (sound of phone being slammed down). My old buddy Ken Levine made the mistake of calling him Bob on the air when they were working together at K-100. He never heard the end of it.

Robert was ultra-sensitive about his name because he'd had to fight like hell to get to use it. The unimaginative management he'd worked for in the past thought that Bob Morgan was just fine, so why change? But Robert was looking to build a brand and the name was a big part of it. Just like Tommy Irwin becoming Shotgun Tom Kelly helped brand me.

He had a point.

Now that I was in L.A., I wanted to get into the voiceover business. I was already doing freelance voice work in San Diego for several clients including the San Diego Chargers,

North County Ford, and many others, and was the station voice for TV and radio stations around the country, including The Mighty 690 in San Diego, The BUZZ in Little Rock, and WFLX, the Fox affiliate in West Palm Beach, Fla. I had friends who were ex-jocks and were now successfully doing voiceover work in Los Angeles, like Neil Ross and Joe Cipriano. They both advised me that I should get into a voiceover workshop first.

Doing commercials and voiceovers in San Diego was one thing, they said, but doing commercials and voiceovers in Los Angeles was a quantum leap; a voiceover workshop would really help. After I completed the workshop, if all went well, I would be able to find an agent. They both recommended Marice Tobias. I joined her workshop and found it quite interesting. It was very different from radio.

In fact, a radio background was a liability. The casting folks and the buyers felt that radio announcers had a phony, "announcer" delivery that wasn't credible. Most of the voiceover audition copy would contain a line in the directions in all caps: "NOT AN ANNOUNCER!"

My friends advised me not to tell anyone I was in radio; just be Tom Irwin and not Shotgun Tom Kelly.

Well, that didn't last too long. I was found out by one of the students, Matt Wright. He said, "You are Shotgun Tom from KRTH 101!" I replied that, yes I was, but that I wanted to keep it on the down-low.

After the workshop was over, Marice suggested we should study one-on-one. I said, "Absolutely!" It turned out she, too, lived in the Park La Brea apartments. I would walk over to her tower apartment and we would study voiceover.

After about five weeks of her training, I made an audition tape directed by Marice and engineered by Tony Pepper. I submitted it to The Tisherman agency. Steve Tisherman and Vanessa Gilbert became my agents.

Trailer/promo legend Don LaFontaine was also represented by Tisherman. One day, Don got sick and they needed somebody to fill in for him as the voice of the TV show "America's Most Wanted." Tisherman recommended me.

I was just supposed to sit in for Don until he got out of the hospital but, sadly, there were complications and Don passed away. I took over his job as the voice of "America's Most Wanted."

Another agent at Tisherman was Ilko Drozdoski, who got me an audition at Warner Bros. for the voice of a disc jockey coming out of a radio in the Denzel Washington movie *Déjà Vu*. My voice was in the movie at the beginning and at the end. I was also the voice for a television show on the Spike Television Network called "1000 Ways to Die."

My voice was also used on a hit record. Through a series of phone calls, my friend Tony Pepper got a call from French dance music producer Fred Falke. He wanted to use my voice to narrate a song of his titled "Radio Days."

How appropriate! Fred allowed me to ad-lib about 90% of my performance, and then he wrote and produced the music around it. The Electronic Dance channel on SiriusXM plays it every so often, and it gets played in dance clubs around the world.

Watch the Fred Falke music video to "Radio Days."

I was also invited to appear on camera on the show "Storage Wars" on A&E TV. Darrell and Brandon Sheets came into the studio with some radio-related items for an episode of the show. We had so much fun, but I may have over-estimated the value of the audio console. You can check out the "Storage Wars" clip here:

Watch Shotgun Tom's appearance on the reality TV show "Storage Wars."

And then there was the time I showed up on the show "TMZ"! I was on the air at K-Earth, minding my own business, when out of the blue my cell phone starts blowing up with calls and text messages from my friends on the East Coast: "You're on TMZ!" How could I be on TMZ? I hadn't done anything outrageous or scandalous? Well, I hadn't, but rapper Machine Gun Kelly had, and the on-air crew at TMZ had a little fun with our shared stage names.

As my time at KRTH was just beginning, Robert W. Morgan's time on this earth was drawing to a close.

Weakened by the cancer that would eventually claim his life,

Catch Shotgun Tom and rapper Machine Gun Kelly appearing in the same episode on TMZ.

he had been broadcasting from his house with Jim Carson helping out at the studio along with Robert's sidekick, Joni Caryl. Robert passed away on May 22, 1998.

Now Steele and Morgan were both gone. It seemed like the end of an era.

I would like to add that just recently, we lost another great radio personality. Jim Carson passed away on December 29, 2023. I have many fond memories of Jim, following him Monday-Friday on KRTH for 20 years. Of course, I recall listening to Jim when he was on Boss Radio KGB for many years.

My wife Linda and her friend Jackie worked with Jim at KGB and recall the happy radio days they all spent together at 4141 Pacific Highway in San Diego, the home of Boss Radio KGB.

We attended Jim's memorial in Simi Valley in January 2024, and we were amazed that 300 of his friends and family were in attendance. That shows just how much Jim was loved and will be missed.

Program Director Mike Phillips went to work on the huge task of finding a new morning personality for KRTH. Legendary DJs such as Dan Ingram, Dave Diamond, Charlie Tuna and

Charlie Van Dyke each went on K-Earth for a week, while Mike listened. Eventually Mike picked Charlie Van Dyke.

Charlie Van Dyke's K-Earth morning stint was relatively brief. He already had a hugely successful business voicing imaging tracks and promos for hundreds of TV and radio stations around the country.

It all proved to be too much, and Charlie decided to leave K-Earth and go back to Scottsdale, Arizona to concentrate on his business. The search for a morning jock for KRTH 101 began anew.

Eventually Mike heard about this outstanding morning man in Seattle named Gary Bryan and offered him mornings on KRTH. Gary accepted. He sounded great right from the get-go.

As of this writing Gary and his sidekick Lisa Stanley have been at KRTH 101 for more than 20 years. And to this day, they both can boast a very highly rated morning show.

Mike Phillips was a genius when it came to putting together fun contests on the station. We had the Calendar Girl contest, Money Music Marathon and the Cash Call Jackpot, just to name a few. The contests were fun, and we gave away lots of money.

The listeners loved it!

In 2005, Mike decided to retire and left KRTH in the hands of assistant Program Director Jay Coffey. The search got underway for the new PD. When there's a change in program directors at a radio station, it can sometimes lead to big upheavals. I was a little concerned, but very quickly I got lucky.

For several years, L.A. talk show host Tom Leykis hosted a big Thanksgiving bash at his place in the Hollywood Hills. I am lucky enough to have been a guest a number of times. I attended Tom's Thanksgiving get-together in 2005 and one of his other guests was KOST FM's program director, Jhani Kaye. He'd been keeping KOST at the top of the ratings since 1982 and was one of the most respected programmers in the country.

Jhani and I hit it off. And, to my surprise, he indicated an interest in coming to KRTH. He was fine where he was, he said, but he'd always been a fan of KRTH and would relish the challenge of programming the station. This sounded like a win-win to me.

I liked Jhani and it seemed that he liked me. I was sure he would do a great job at KRTH, so I decided to let KRTH management know about his interest. They quickly contacted Jhani and a deal was put together.

Jhani Kaye, like Mike Phillips, was a very innovative and creative person. He was the perfect fit for KRTH. He came up with the idea of giving away trips for two to Hawaii. We would give away a trip to Hawaii every week, and then every six months, Jhani would have me do the show live from one of the Hawaiian Islands.

These vacation giveaways continued for several years, and KRTH 101 became known as your Hawaiian vacation station.

One of my contestants was Hollywood television and movie

producer and director Allen Brent Connell. Allen won a trip for two to Hawaii, and we became fast friends. I had other winners who worked in Hollywood and won trips to Hawaii like Tony Carciopplo and Ken Karagozian, who worked over at the ABC television network.

Over at the Paramount lot, my friend Aaron Segal, who is considered the honorary mayor of Paramount Studios and runs the Water Tower Cafe, was also one of my listeners. He made sure that my picture was up on the wall at the café on the Paramount lot.

One year, the KRTH Christmas party was held at Vibroto Jazz Grill in Beverly Hills, owned by Herb Alpert. As I walked into the party, I saw Clint Eastwood and a friend seated at one of the tables.

At first, I didn't want to intrude, which is highly unusual for me (I'm kidding!), but Clint caught my eye and so I decided to go over and introduce myself.

I said "Mr. Eastwood, I'm Shotgun Tom Kelly," and before I could go on Clint said, "I know who you are, I listen to you on KRTH." He then said, "This is my friend, Tom Dreesen."

Then Tom piped up and said he also listened to me. I knew who Tom Dreesen was, being a Frank Sinatra fan. Tom was the longtime warm-up comedian for Frank's concerts, as well as a frequent guest on the "Tonight Show."

We began talking about jazz music and our mutual favorite jazz radio personality, Chuck Niles. Clint was delighted to hear that I was a good friend of Chuck.

As I was speaking and trying to make a point about how much I loved jazz, I began to gesture with my hands. Unfortunately, Clint's wine glass got in my way. I knocked the glass over and before I could stop it from falling, it spilled on the tablecloth. Fortunately, the glass did not hold wine, but, rather, a small amount of water. Thank goodness for that! After my apologies, Clint exclaimed, "Whoa, I'm not riding *shotgun* with you!" We all had a good laugh.

Every year Gary Bryan and his sidekick, Lisa Stanley, would bring Stevie Wonder on the show to promote Stevie's House Full of Toys concert, which benefits children, people with disabilities and families in need.

Gary would always invite me to join him on the air in the morning with Stevie. Stevie's brother, Milton Hardaway, would always come along. He's a great guy and we are friends to this day.

When my daughter, Melanie, was graduating from San Diego State University with a B.S. in nursing, I told Stevie that when Melanie was born, to celebrate her birth, I had played Stevie's song "Isn't She Lovely" on my show. So Stevie and his brother Milton went back to Stevie's studio and recorded something for her.

We played it at her graduation dinner. I got Melanie up on stage and cued the audio guy and out of the speakers came: "Hi Melanie, this is Stevie on behalf of your father, congratulating you on your graduation from the San Diego State University School of Nursing, what can I say?" And he sang, "Isn't She Lovely."

There wasn't a dry eye in the room.

This next story is so unbelievable, but I swear it's true. In order to tell it I have to hit the rewind button and take us back to my days on KCBQ in San Diego. I was working afternoon drive and we had a lot of contest giveaways. One afternoon the prize was the *Chicago VI* album. So I went on the air and said, "Caller number six wins the *Chicago VI* LP. Call now!!

I answered the phone. "KCBQ, you are caller number six. Who's this?"

"My name is Jason."

"Well, Jason, you just won the Chicago VI LP – congratulations to you!!"

Jason thanked me and I asked him what he did and he said that he had a little rock 'n' roll band and that he played bass.

I said, "That's great!! Maybe someday you'll be on stage playing bass with Chicago!"

Jason said he hoped so, and with that, our call ended.
Now flash forward 30 years and KRTH brings Chicago to Irvine Meadows for a concert. The DJs are backstage getting their pictures taken with the band and one of the group members approached me and said, "We gotta get on stage now but I want to talk to you, so don't go anywhere!"

I told him I wouldn't.

So I'm watching the show and I see this guy on stage singing and playing his bass. I was sitting next to KTLA's Channel 5 morning newsman, Carlos Amezcua, and he told me this guy was named Jason Scheff and that he went to Point Loma High School in San Diego. By now you can begin to see where this is going, but trust me … I was still clueless.

Chicago was winding up their last song, so I stood up from my seat and walked backstage waiting for this guy to come offstage. The first guy off was Robert Lamm, who said, "Hey, Jason wants to talk to you!"

Next off was the horn section, all of whom looked at me as one of them said, "Jason needs to talk to you!"

"I know, I'm not going anywhere."

Finally, Jason came off and said, "Shotgun, I'm so glad you're here! Hey, listen we got to go do an encore, stay right here!"

I assured him I wasn't going anywhere and stood there wondering what the heck he wanted to tell me. I watched Jason sing, "25 or 6 to 4," and he saw me backstage out of the corner of his eye. As he sang the last note of the song, he did the Brrrr-yah sound effect that I do on the radio. I was surprised, to say the least.

Then Jason exited the stage, and there were a bunch of girls backstage clamoring for his attention. (Being a rock star is a tough job, but SOMEBODY has to do it!).

Finally, after the girls left, Jason said to me, "Shotgun, there's no way you'd remember this, but when I was a kid I won a *Chicago VI* album from you on KCBQ and you asked me what I did and I told you I was in a little rock 'n' roll band and I played bass and then you said, 'Well who knows, maybe one

Photo from Irwin Family Archives

Shotgun Tom and Jason Scheff on
"On the Air with Sully and Little Tommy."

day you'll be on stage playing bass with Chicago.'"

I had totally forgotten that, of course, but it stuck in his mind. Because of me, he said, he learned all the Chicago songs and grew very interested in the band.

One thing led to another and eventually my little whimsical throw-away line came true. Jason served as lead vocalist and bassist for Chicago for 25 years!

I told that story on San Diego's KUSI-TV's "On the Air" show in San Diego, and Jason was the featured guest. He did three songs on the show and when he sang "Feeling Stronger Every Day," he did the "Shotgun Tom" sound two times in the song and threw in the KCBQ call letters too!

I had been out of the San Diego radio market for nearly

20 years, but I still received invitations to make personal appearances in San Diego on occasion. The summer following my star ceremony, I was asked to introduce one of my favorite recording artists, Huey Lewis, at the San Diego County Fair in Del Mar.

When Linda and I arrived, we were escorted backstage. Linda was standing next to Huey Lewis while I walked on stage. I started by introducing myself to the audience and before I could begin my Huey Lewis intro, the crowd began standing up, cheering and calling my name.

I was blown away. I truly didn't think the San Diego crowd remembered me. Just then Huey turned to Linda and said, "Wow, they sure do like Shotgun Tom."

Linda smiled and replied, "Well, of course. This is his hometown!!!" Of all the times I've been on stage introducing countless recording artists, that experience still stands out in both our minds as one of the most memorable.

I had a great run on KRTH 101. I had some pretty amazing experiences and met many, many wonderful people. The high point, of course, was getting my star on the Hollywood Walk of Fame.

You remember me getting the star on the Hollywood Walk of Fame, right?

But two months after that wonderful day, Jhani Kaye announced that he was retiring from the station. There would be a new program director. Remember what I said about new PDs?

My ninth contract with the station was up and it was time for renewal. The new program director and the general manager invited me to lunch at a restaurant across the street to discuss things. This was the way renewals were usually handled. No red flags yet.

We sat down at a table and right away the GM said, "Hey, Shotgun, we're giving you a promotion! We're going to take you off afternoon drive and make you the Ambassador of KRTH! You can do personal appearances for the station and do one weekend show."

He also mentioned there'd be a sizeable pay cut. Some "promotion"! I sat there in shock.

The food came and I couldn't eat it. The waiter asked if there was a problem with my lunch. I replied the food was fine; the only problem was that I was in the process of getting fired! I took the deal, but it was a bitter pill. And it only lasted a year before they let me go.

It was time to give notice at Park La Brea and head back to San Diego.

Watch a 2005 clip of Shotgun Tom broadcasting at K-Earth 101.

Jack And The Pool Hall

At this point I want to stop the story for a moment and tell you about one of my favorite places to be and one of my dearest friends ever.

My friend is Jack Vincent and the place is my pool hall, a makeshift gathering spot in my garage. There probably wouldn't be a pool hall without Jack, so let's start with him.

John Vincent Oatsdean was born on November 7, 1917 in Youngstown, Ohio. He did a stint in the Marine Corps during World War II, and when he mustered out in 1946, he found work in heavy construction. One of the projects he worked on was the Hoover Dam. Doesn't get much heavier than that!

That might have been the end of the story, but fate reared its head. At the age of 34 Jack suffered a work-related back injury that pretty much took him out of the construction game. While searching around for something less strenuous to do, he remembered a brief exposure he'd had to radio in high school and decided to give that a try.

A stint at a radio trade school, courtesy of the G.I. Bill, gave him some announcing skills and, perhaps more importantly, a first-class FCC license. In short order, Jack (now using the name Jack Vincent) landed a job at KXO in El Centro, California. All went well until Jack experienced his first scalding hot El Centro summer. He vowed it would be his last. He was able to land a job in the relatively cooler clime of San Bernardino, where he worked at KFXM.

Still, Jack and his wife found themselves longing to be in San Diego, and in 1955, Jack joined the staff of KCBQ in San Diego as an engineer. It wasn't long before he was back on the air. The station's all-night DJ went on vacation and Jack was tapped to fill in. He did such a good job that he ended up being given the show, where he remained for the next 13 years.

KCBQ's headquarters consisted of a glassed-in studio and offices at 7th and Ash in downtown San Diego, which I've told you about, but Jack didn't work there. The all-night DJ at KCBQ performed what was called a combo job. In addition to spinning tunes, Jack would also be responsible for monitoring and maintaining the station's transmitter and complicated six-tower transmission array. He would do all of this from a studio at the station's transmitter site in Santee, then little more than a wide spot in the road about 10 miles northeast of downtown San Diego.

The all-night show in radio is a great place to hide — especially if you're not broadcasting from the main studio. You don't have to deal with management, and you don't get caught up in inter-office politics. If you show up on time and keep the station on the air, they leave you alone and don't mess with you.

Photo from Irwin Family Archives

Jack Vincent, on the air.

To give you an idea of how insulated Jack was from the day-to-day shenanigans at the station, he once told us an interesting story.

Things went a bit crazy for a while, and in rapid succession, the station rolled through five different program directors, none of whom Jack actually met.

When the sixth guy was installed, Jack signed off the air one morning, drove downtown and had breakfast. Then, at 9 a.m., he walked into the station's downtown facility, marched into the program director's office, stuck out his hand and said,

"Hi! I'm your overnight man, Jack Vincent. I missed the last five program directors, so I thought I'd better come in and meet you!"

It also didn't hurt that then-KCBQ owner Lee Bartell had a genuine affection for Jack and would put up with the occasional bit of insubordination.

Photo from Irwin Family Archives

Jack Vincent portrait.

Like the night Jack got so sick of the Top 40 music he had to play (which he secretly detested) that he spent an entire show playing nothing but Dixieland jazz. Kind of a shock for the teeny boppers.

When he got wind of it, Mr. Bartell let Jack know that he'd overlook it this one time, but there had better not be a next time!

Most guys would have been fired.

Jack bore an AMAZING resemblance to Hollywood movie star Clark Gable. The resemblance between him and Rhett Butler from *Gone With the Wind* was astonishing. They could've been brothers!

Jack also possessed a smooth baritone voice that sounded like it was sweetened with honey, soothing and friendly, not loud and flashy like a lot of his Top 40 brethren. That gentle voice guided listeners through the wee small hours of the morning.

I first became aware of Jack's voice when I was 13 and listening to KCBQ in bed late at night on my pocket transistor radio. Somehow, I found out Jack was broadcasting from the Santee transmitter site, which wasn't too far from where I lived.

Shortly thereafter, I landed at an early morning newspaper delivery route and listened to Jack as I folded and delivered the *San Diego Union* to my customers. After I'd delivered all my papers, I would bike over to Santee to see Jack. He would leave the door open for me, and we became friends.

Other radio friends visited Jack, including Bill Lipis, Mike

Moyes, and Bill Martin. Jack would always leave the door open for us. As I got older and started working at KPRI FM in 1966, I met one of the other KPRI jocks, Bob Neutzling and his wife, Linda. We all would visit Jack.

Jack was the first radio pro who took me seriously and told me that I could make it in radio. That was such a great thing to hear! He also emphasized the importance of securing that first-class FCC license and told me about Bill Ogden.

Jack and I lost touch as my career got underway and I bounced around in the smaller markets. But when I returned to San Diego and went to work for KCBQ, I was delighted to find Jack still at the station. He was off the air now and working in the engineering department, but our friendship really jelled. We remained pals from then on.

It was Jack who came up with the pool hall idea. When I started to work in Los Angeles, I worried about losing all my San Diego buddies, so I decided to start inviting them up to my place in El Cajon on Saturday nights to hang out. I ran the idea by Jack and he didn't think that would work.

"If guys tell their wives they're going to your place to hang out, the ladies won't go for it," Jack opined. "They need to say they're going to be doing some kind of activity. I suggest you put a pool table in your garage so they can tell the wives they're coming to shoot pool. That'll work."

Tony Pepper, Jack Vincent, and I started playing pool on the weekends and eventually would invite other people to come over and play pool with us. That was actually the start of the pool hall.

The only problem? My pool table wasn't very good. My friend Kirby Winn had given it to me. It was fine for a free table, but it just wasn't good enough for the pool hall I had in mind.

Jack had made a beautiful pool room clock for his house on Mount Helix. He used pool balls for the numbers and pool cue sticks for the hands. I always admired the clock and Jack knew it. He said, "If you get a slate top pool table, I will give you that clock."

Deal!

I went up to Olhausen Billiards, and I saw a beautiful, slate top pool table called The Championship Pro, the kind of pool table used in tournaments on ESPN. I asked Gloria at Olhausen about the price. "Five thousand out the door," she said.

Excited, I approached Linda and said I wanted to buy a pool table for $5,000. She simply said, "Nothing doing!"

I had to resort to Plan B.

I got together with Tony Pepper and we recorded a spec commercial for Olhausen Billiards. I played the commercial on my Boombox for the owner, Butch Olhausen, and his general manager. They liked it and asked, "How much will this commercial cost us?"

"I've always wanted a championship pro pool table."

"Is that all you want?" asked Butch.

A week later, the pool table was delivered! Jack was so happy he gave me his beautiful poolroom clock, which hangs on my pool room wall to this day.

Our pool hall gatherings originally started on Saturday nights. We would pick up Jack Vincent at his apartment and bring him to my place. Then some of the regulars would start to arrive: Jeff Prescott, John Fewel, Todd Williams, Tony Pepper, Marty Levine and his friend Terry, Frank Anthony, Mel Hall, John Polo, Chuck Karazsia, John Tenwolde, Wes Owen, Chris Carmichael, Russ T. Nailz, Steve Blessing, Joe Nelson, Dave Grudt, Scottie Rice, Gilbert Smith and Fred Bushardt. Not too many ladies joined us, except for Karen Beth Pearlman, a writer for the *San Diego Union*. And, of course, Linda.

Some of the guests who came less frequently, mostly due to geography, included the very talented voice-over guy Neil Ross; ex-KCBQ newsman Lee Marshall, who was now the voice of Tony the Tiger following the retirement of Thurl Ravenscroft; and Chuck McCann, the voice of the Cocoa Puffs toucan bird and many other commercials. Other less frequent guests included talk show maven Tom Leykis; Larry "Motormouth" Huffman, the guy who talked me out of quitting Ogden's all those years ago; San Diego Police Chief Bill Kolender; San Diego Sheriff John Duffy; Santee Mayor Randy Voepel; and longtime lead singer for the rock group Chicago, Jason Scheff.

John Fewel connected us with his brother, Dan Mills, a really talented artist specializing in caricatures. We asked him to create some portraits of the "pool hall punks," as we called ourselves. The amazing thing is Dan had never met any of us, except John, of course. We simply sent him a photograph of one of us, and a while later, received the finished caricature. It's astonishing what Dan was able to do with just one photograph. Even though he didn't know the guys, he still manages to capture their essence. Those wonderful caricatures remain on display in the pool hall and we always held a little ceremony every time we added a new one.

Eventually the pool hall transitioned into the pool/train hall. My interest in model trains began when I was six years old. When I asked my parents about it, my dad had refused. I can't say as I blamed him. After all, working 16 hours a day, the last thing he'd want to see at home was a trains.

So, I waited until just before I left KRTH and asked Lloyd and Betsy Kluesner of Lloyd's Layouts to build a train layout for me. It took them a year and a half, and they did a beautiful job.

My layout consists of a downtown area, which has an AM FM-TV station, along with a train yard and four industrial areas. I also have a residential area backdropped by a mountain, where my television tower is. My AM radio tower stands by the 'river'. My radio and television call letters are KOS.

Along with these features, I have several custom buildings on my layout that are personal to me. My friend John Fewel used to be a car salesman, so the car dealership is called John Fewel Motors: "Where all cars are delivered as is."

I even have the KOS Radio mobile studio, a ringer for the studio where Frank Thompson put me on the radio for the first time. My vehicles include a replica of Broderick Crawford's Highway Patrol car, the Oscar Meyer Wiener Mobile, my dad's 2357 switch engine, and his 347 red War Bonnet Santa Fe passenger train.

I'll dive into more detail on my train setup in Chapter 25.

The train layout sits on my pool table. When we want to play pool, I press a button and the layout lifts up from the pool table and disappears into the rafters. The pool lights appear from the bottom of the layout, and we're ready to shoot some pool.

Despite what we told the wives, I must confess that over time more and more socializing happened at the pool hall, which led to less and less billiards being played.

Radio guys seem to have an endless supply of stories, and they are very good story tellers. Some tales are absolutely hilarious, others fascinating, but they're seldom dull.

Obviously, over the years I've had so much fun and fellowship at the pool hall. It's good for the soul.

Besides our weekly "pool" parties, we also hosted a yearly party during my Modern Oldies days, which became a Christmas Eve tradition. Linda was employed as the traffic manager for KCBQ AM, which was now doing sports programming after years as a Top 40 station.

We were both back at the ranch house again. This time, though, would be our last KCBQ experience.

That first Christmas, we realized that both Jeff Stewart and Rich Brother Robbin did not have family in town, so Linda and I invited them, and a few other friends, to celebrate Christmas Eve with us. The following year, a few more friends were added to the list. Among the invitees were our very close friends Bill Martin, Bill Lipis, Phyllis and John Achuff (Linda and Phyllis actually met while working at none other than KCBQ AM in the Seventies).

The Christmas Eve parties started out with about eight people, then somehow, through word of mouth, we ended up hosting as many as 60 to 70. One year, one of our guests was the very talented two-time Grammy Award winner Dianne Shuur. The big band vocalist treated all of us to a mini performance directly from our living room, which was aired live on our local channel KUSI TV. Dave Scott, the weather reporter, was on hand to do the local weather (using the lovely outdoor Christmas decorations set up by our next-door neighbors Mary and Jerry Howe as the backdrop).

Following the weather report, Dave conducted an on-air interview with Diane. By the way, Dave is a jazz musician in his own right. He sings and plays the trombone weekly around San Diego. Every other week he appears at Hacienda Casa Blanca in El Cajon, a San Diego suburb just east of where we live. I enjoy going there and having a tasty meal while listening to my talented friend.

Our Christmas Eve party tradition lasted well over 10 years until it became too much of an undertaking. The last straw was the year one of the "guests" (we had no idea who he was or who invited him) showed up with a parrot perched on his shoulder. As he walked around the house with his parrot, you can guess what a mess the parrot was making. We decided to nix the Christmas Eve parties and hang out with our good friends, the Achuffs, during the holidays. That tradition has lasted to this day.

A Monumental Experience

Our house in San Diego was only a few minutes away from the KCBQ studios, offices and transmitter in Santee.

Almost every weekend, I'd drive past it, and even though it had new owners and was broadcasting a talk format, just seeing it always brought back wonderful memories of one of the happiest times in my life. But by 2008, those memories looked like they'd soon be harder to come by.

Amazingly enough, KCBQ never owned the land on which it sat for more than a half century. I guess back in the Fifties and Sixties, when Santee was just a rural outpost, it didn't cost much for the station to lease the land.

But as the years rolled by, developers started building housing, and people started buying those houses. By 2020, Santee's population had ballooned to over 60,000, with plenty of shopping centers and big box stores to serve those folks.

In 2008, KCBQ radio was worth far less than the land. The owners decided to use the property for a shopping center and declined to renew the station's lease. KCBQ would have to find a new home.

The studios and the transmitters were the first to go. Then the bulldozers arrived. Down came the buildings, then the six iconic towers. The land was leveled and, as shopping center construction began, it was hard to believe the station had ever been there.

Linda and I were understandably saddened. One day, talking about it with our friend Chris Carmichael, we came up with an idea for a monument that would tell people now and in the future about the station and what it had meant to the community.

If I'd had any idea then what we were getting into, I might not have even started.

It seemed like a simple enough project, though: design a monument and install it on the grass strip in front of the shopping center between the sidewalk and the street. The city would own that strip and give us permission and ... easy-peasy, right?

If I shared with you all the hoops we had to jump through, this would be a much longer book. I almost gave up several times, but we had a great ally in state Assemblyman Randy Voepel, Santee's mayor at the time. He thought the monument was a great idea and went to bat for us, running interference countless times as we hacked through the bureaucratic jungle.

We put together a committee consisting of former KCBQ employees and folks who had been long-time fans of the station. Funds needed to be raised and we put out the word to everyone we could think of who might want to contribute.

The money began to come in. Some former employees were quite generous. Others, due to their circumstances, could only chip in a little; some, not at all. One ex-employee sent a check for $50. But it was contingent upon us agreeing to a specific placement for his name, the size of the letters and the font. Linda sent his check back, telling him we were sorry, but we would not be able to accommodate him.

The design of the monument gradually began to materialize. The top part would feature a picture of the station and a brief written history. The lower portion would consist of a plaque with the names of all the folks who had been on the air during the station's Top 40 heyday from 1958 to 1978.

Assembling the list of names was daunting in and of itself. We formed a committee and spread the word. Names began to come in. A lot of broadcast talent had graced the studios of KCBQ during the station's 20 years of Top 40 dominance. We didn't want to list anybody who didn't belong, but we were also terrified of leaving somebody out who did. How do you whittle it down while making sure everyone who made a vital contribution was duly honored?

Some names popped up that, unfortunately, did not bring back happy memories. Broadcasters can be volatile people, and a lot of us have outsized egos. Sometimes there was friction, which happened when one name was brought up, a guy with whom I'd had problems. "I don't want him on the monument," I said. "He's an asshole!"

At the other end of the table committee member Neil Ross quietly responded, "Tom, if we eliminate all the assholes, there won't be any names up there at all, mine included."

Neil had a point.

As the day of the unveiling approached, we did our best to get the word out, using newspapers, the internet, and yours truly appearing on as many local San Diego TV newscasts as I possibly could. Still, when Saturday, August 28, 2010, arrived and Linda and I got in the car for the short drive to the monument site, we couldn't help but wonder if all we'd see was an empty parking lot. So many years had elapsed since the glory years of KCBQ radio.

Would anybody remember? Would anybody care?

Happily, our fears proved unfounded. The parking lot that faced the monument was jammed with people. The turnout was just great, and it was truly a beautiful day as fans of the station mingled with their favorite DJs and news people, sharing stories, laughter and love.

Watch the video of the KCBQ memorial ceremony.

We began the ceremony with a number of speakers, including ex-KCBQ newsman Lee Marshall, Neil Ross, Santee Mayor Randy Voepel and prominent San Diego hotel owner Richard Bartell, the son of former KCBQ owner Lee Bartell. Linda and I spent a few minutes at the microphone, too.

Then it was time to build up to the unveiling, I read the names on the monument. It was very emotional, but I managed to keep my composure until I read the name Don Howard.

Don was the midday DJ on KCBQ when I was a kid, and we later became friends. He was a great guy who in many ways had been a mentor to me. I wished he could have been there that day, but he'd passed away some years previously.

When I said his name, I began to cry, and the catch in my

Photo by Tony Pepper

Shotgun Tom with Jack Vincent
at the unveiling of the KCBQ monument.

Photo by Tony Pepper

The KCBQ monument top.

voice was audible. After I regained my composure, Linda and I, Mayor Voepel, Richard Bartell and the living legend, Jack Vincent, unveiled the monument and the crowd surged forward.

All our hard work was worth it. Saturday, August 28, 2010, was one of the greatest days I ever experienced. Remembering all the joy and happiness around me that day still gives a me warm feeling. I invite you to take in the experience with this excellent video (see page 208), hosted by my longtime DJ buddy Bobby Ocean. It captures all the wonderful events of the day.

Photo by Tony Pepper

The entire KCBQ monument.

Swingin' On A Satellite

After I left KRTH, I was off the air for a little more than a year. Friends kept asking what I was going to do next. Look for another radio job in Los Angeles or San Diego, maybe?

No, my next goal was higher than that. Sky high. Maybe even higher.

On March 18, 2001, a year better known in media technology for Apple's introduction of the iPod, another monumental moment took place.

A satellite nicknamed "Rock" and built by Boeing Satellite Systems was launched into geosynchronous orbit some 24,800 miles over North America.

A second satellite, dubbed "Roll," followed on May 8. With the launches of "Rock" and "Roll" the age of satellite radio had begun. Instead of radiating off an earth-based transmitter and tower, the programming would be fed to one of the orbiting satellites and be beamed back down to earth, where listeners equipped with special receivers could hear it.

This new satellite transmitting technology allowed for a huge number of music channels to broadcast every conceivable genre of music from every era. There would also be news, talk and sports programming. The music channels would also be completely commercial-free.

Rather than enduring numerous 30- and 60-second spots, listeners would pay for a monthly subscription. They'd also have to invest in the equipment to hear the programming.

Millions of people would have to be convinced that it was worth the trouble and expense and car makers would have to be induced to install satellite receivers in the new cars they manufactured. It was a tough sell. Initially there were two satellite radio services, XM and Sirius. XM's first broadcast took place on September 25, 2001. Four months later, Sirius signed on.

It was touch-and-go for a while. A lot of industry observers spent the first half of the new millennium and decade predicting that satellite radio would ultimately fail. Initially, XM was in the lead in the race for subscribers. Then, in a game-changing move, Sirius lured the "King of All Media", Shock Talk maestro Howard Stern, away from terrestrial radio. Overnight, the tide turned. Eventually Sirius swallowed up XM to become the satellite radio megalith we know today as SiriusXM. Satellite radio was here to stay.

That's where I wanted to work.

Remember the interview I conducted with reporter Cathy Clark talking about what a rush it was to have my voice come out of a transmitter, go up a tower and blast out all over the city?

If that was a rush, imagine what I thought about my voice shooting up into space and being blasted down to a nationwide audience! A worldwide audience, if you include subscribers listening online. That's a rush squared! I set to work trying to make it happen.

But there was one problem: there were no openings. Lou Simon, now running The Jukebox Diner on SiriusXM, had been a longtime friend. We used to listen to Lou when he was on The Fabulous 690, a high-powered Mexican station broadcasting in English from Rosarito Beach.

Lou was not only very listenable with his engaging radio personality, but he was also able to bring the recording artists and their music to life with his compelling and ultra-smooth style. Linda and I thought he sounded a lot like our old friend Don Howard, one of the original KCBQ DJs.

We met Lou in Avalon on Catalina Island at a Fabulous 690 promotional event. The station was soon to switch back to Spanish-language programming, much to our disappointment, and we asked Lou what his next plans might be.

He mentioned he'd love to program an oldies format, which is exactly where he landed. Lou went on to program several channels on SiriusXM, including the 60s Gold channel. Along with his programming duties, Lou still hosts "Jukebox Diner" on Sunday evenings on the 60s Gold Channel.

Give a listen and you're sure to be thoroughly entertained.

When I left KRTH, several people, including Art Vuolo, "Radio's Best Friend," suggested to Lou that he bring me on the 60s Gold channel. Lou said that he certainly wanted to, but there were no openings.

About two years later, I popped into the SiriusXM studio on Wilshire Boulevard in L.A. to see the facility and say hi to a few employees I knew. While there, I was introduced to a guy named Kid Kelly.

I'd never met him, but I'd sure heard about him. He'd built a huge career back East, including two stints in the Big Apple. We talked about his career and we hit it off. I told him of my interest of being on the 60s Gold channel but, like Lou, Kid said, "We'd love to have you but there's just no openings."

More time passed. One day, attending a media luncheon in Los Angeles honoring Regis Philbin, yet another legendary broadcaster who first built a name in San Diego, I received a call from Kid Kelly. At long last, he told me, there was a rare opening. Would I like to join the 60s Gold channel?

"Yes!" Kid told me to call Lou Simon.

Lou was ready for my call. He informed me that I would be voice tracking my show from my home studio, and then he put me in touch with SiriusXM's IT guy, Jinx, in Washington D.C., who helped me with the technical set up on my end.

For the next week, I practiced being on the Sixties channel, to get the hang of voice tracking. Lou Simon and Kid Kelly came up with a start date of Labor Day 2018.

Another nice surprise for me when I joined SiriusXM occurred when old friend and fellow Sixties channel DJ Pat St. John called to congratulate me.

While we talked, Pat added that Jeremy Savage wanted to welcome me to SiriusXM too. I didn't remember the name, but I gave Jeremy a call anyway.

When we spoke, Jeremy wanted to tell me a story.

Photo by Tony Pepper

Shotgun Tom celebrating his 70th birthday at a pool hall party with the Famous Chicken and Pat St. John of SiriusXM.

"I was in San Diego wanting to get into radio in 1976. I went to a radio station where there was an all-night DJ named Jeff Rew. Jeff told me he was a longtime friend of Shotgun Tom and that you and he had worked together at KPRI FM."

Jeff was a professional studio musician who played stand-up bass on many recording sessions. The all-night jazz show at KFSD was just a side hustle. "When Jeff got off the air, we went over and visited you at B-100 FM," Jeremy continued. "That was the first time I ever saw a high-energy Top 40 DJ at work. I was so impressed!"

Jeremy went on to tell me that he had played me his audition tape and that I'd made some suggestions for changes, which he followed. That tape resulted in his first radio job.

He had gradually shifted over to the technical side and was now one of the top engineers at SiriusXM.

Jeremy said he'd never forgotten my kindness, and wanted me to know if I ever had any tech problems or questions to just pick up the phone. It's nice to know I have a new friend to guide me through the sometimes-befuddling digital world!

So, I happily settled into life on the SiriusXM Sixties channel. After a year on the beach, as we say in the business, it was so great to be back on the air entertaining a nationwide (worldwide, thanks to the internet) audience. I still feel that excitement to this very day!

Following Lou Simon's promotion to vice president of music programming, Brian DeNicola became program director of the Sixties, Seventies, and Sinatra channels. Brian previously worked with Cousin Brucie.

I appreciate Brian. He's always helpful. For example, if there's a requested song I'm having difficulty finding for my listener, he digs into the archive and makes it available.

And it's not only Brian that I appreciate, because I get to work with a lot of great people at SiriusXM on 60s Gold, including:

- Phlash Phelps, who is our morning host and resident "Road" Scholar. He has visited all 50 states more than once;

- Dave Hoeffel, who does mid-days and hosts The 60s Satellite Survey;

- Pat St. John. The man is a living radio legend and member of the Radio Hall of Fame. I'm thrilled to have him as my lead in;

- Mike Kelly, who is on Saturday and Sunday sharing his love of the 60s car culture; and

- Bond Collard, who – as our coordinator – keeps us all up to date about what's happening on the channel.

We are one big radio family, and I consider myself to be very fortunate to be a part of it.

Watch a video of Shotgun on the air on SiriusXM.

Beyond The Airwaves

During the COVID-19 era in 2020, my longtime friend Little Tommy Sablan contacted me and asked if I would like to be a guest on a new show on KUSI TV called "On The Air with Sully and Little Tommy." I was a little apprehensive, as were many, about being around groups of people. I declined.

When the show aired a couple of weeks later on a Saturday morning, I was extremely impressed with the hosts, guests, and the production. It was very entertaining.

The hosts, Robert "Sully" Sullivan, Russ T. Nailz, and Little Tommy, played off one another perfectly. The show had great continuity and flow. It's just so great to see such a professionally produced show on a local TV station! Sully, one of the originators of "On the Air," worked at several radio stations in San Diego as their business reporter. He is the host of the nationally syndicated TV program, "The Big

Biz Show." Sully also designed the "On the Air" set to his specifications. I think it's one of the best television studios I've ever seen.

Not only is Sully fabulous as one of the hosts, but he has his own band, in which he is the guitarist. He's quite a good singer, too. The Sully Band is featured on the "On the Air" weekly show. All the musicians are incredibly talented. The band often performs at the Belly Up Tavern in Solana Beach, a North County suburb of San Diego, and also around town at many charity events.

Anyhow, the persistent Little Tommy called me again and asked if I was willing to be on the show. This time I accepted, but decided to wear a mask. I removed it at the start of the show when the guys began to chide me about it. If being a guest over 14 times says anything about how much I enjoy being on their show, then I don't know what does.

I truly love being among their many guests, which have also included the Famous San Diego Chicken; our former San Diego mayor and talk show host, Roger Hedgecock; various San Diego radio personalities such as Eddie Papani (Rock 105.3 KIOZ FM), Jesse Lozano, Tati and Delana (Star 94.1 KMYI FM), Clint August (Classic Rock 101.5 KGB FM), and LaDonna Harvey (KOGO AM); sports celebrities; chiefs of police; musicians; and so many other interesting members of our San Diego community.

"On the Air" is extremely successful. I can't tell you how many people come up to me and tell me how much they love watching this locally produced show. In the spring of 2022, a tragic event occurred during the taping of the show. Russ

T. Nailz, the Emmy Award-winning DJ and comedian, was beautifully performing the song "I Melt with You" by Modern English. Immediately after he finished the song, with a smile still on his face, he fell off the stage and landed in my lap.

At first, thinking his fall was part of his comedic act, I began to laugh. But within seconds, all of us realized that he was not being funny and was in dire trouble. One of the band members stepped in immediately and began CPR until the paramedics arrived.

Russ was rushed to the ER, but sadly passed away a few hours later with his family members by his side, the victim of a ruptured aortic aneurysm, a bulge in the wall of the main artery taking blood from your heart to the rest of your body.

Russ T. Nailz was extremely talented. He could play his guitar and sing almost any genre from rock to country and more. And his impressions of celebrities were spot on.

He had the uncanny ability to delight his audiences whenever he was on stage. He performed at countless charitable organizations in and around San Diego, donating his talent to the community. He is missed not only by his family and friends, but by all of San Diego.

Watch Shotgun Tom's appearance on the March 30, 2024 episode of "On the Air with Sully and Little Tommy."

Although it was very difficult for Sully and Little Tommy to carry on without Russ T. Nailz on board, they have continued to entertain the San Diego audience on Saturdays at 11 a.m. I wouldn't be surprised if Russ T. Nailz isn't looking down on his friends with a smile on his face and a nod of approval.

Long Train Runnin'

You probably remember the story about the time the 8-year-old me came home from school and asked my dad – a real train engineer on the Santa Fe Railroad – if I could have a model train set. He said, "Nothing doing, son. I work 16 hours a day. I don't want to see trains when I come home."

So with that, I put my dream aside – until I became an adult and was able to build one myself.

I know I touched upon this earlier in the book. Now, here's the full story of my train layout.

KRTH program director Jhani Kaye had his own Disneyland train layout. I asked him, "How did you build that?" He told me he didn't build it – he had it built by Lloyd's Layouts, a company near Los Angeles that builds model train layouts professionally. It is owned and operated by a husband-and-wife team, Lloyd and Betsy Kluesner.

So I contacted them and said I would like my own layout. They asked me what I'd like to see, and I presented them with a long list, including a downtown area with a TV and radio broadcast station, a neighborhood with houses, a mountain for my TV tower and a train yard.

Lloyd got on his computer and drew up plans incorporating all my "wants." We went back and forth a few times but ultimately I got the perfect blueprint.

I couldn't wait to see that blueprint materialize into an actual train layout, but Lloyd told me he would put me on a waiting list and that it would take at least a year before he could even get started. He had a couple of clients before me.

At that point, all I could do was dream and get my model train fix by going around to some of my favorite train stores, like Reed's in La Mesa, California, near my home, and Arnie's Trains in Westminster, California.

Greg Arnold is the owner of Arnie's Trains, and his general manager is Kevin Honda. One day, Kevin asked if I wanted to come over to his house and see his layout and run some trains while waiting for my layout to be built. I took him up on his kind offer.

He has a shelf layout in his garage, and it is absolutely beautiful. The scenery is perfect. He taught me how to run and switch trains. We had a great time, and it was the start of a wonderful friendship.

Soon thereafter, I found Jeff Smith's Railmaster Hobbies in Bellflower, another L.A. suburb. That's where I bought my very first Santa Fe switch engine for my new layout.

It was an Atlas product with my dad's train number: 2357. I couldn't believe I found the same number as my dad's on a model switch engine. They only had two left. I didn't want to be greedy, so I only bought one.

I should have bought the other one, as well. With model railroad products in limited production, if you see something you want and there are only two of them, you had better buy them both now or you won't be able to find them in the future. I thought about going back and acquiring the other one, but when I finally made the trip back up to Railmaster Hobbies, it was gone. Someone else had bought it. I was out of luck.

I took my new 2357 Santa Fe switch engine to Kevin Honda. It was DC, but my new layout was going to be DCC, so Kevin had to work his magic to put a new DCC sound card in the engine. I took it out for a test run, and it ran beautifully. "Shotgun, this is going to be your favorite engine," he said.

Kevin was right – it is my favorite. It's my favorite because it was my dad's switch engine and number. It meant a lot to me. I started buying more trains, including my dad's red 347C Santa Fe "Warbonnet" F7 along with the B unit and all the passenger cars.

Watch Shotgun Tom riding his dad's red Santa Fe "Warbonnet" engine.

I still didn't have a layout, so where was I going to run the trains that I had purchased? I met a guy named Michael Benjamin one day while hanging around at Arnie's Trains.

He said he was a member of the San Diego Model Railroad Museum, which is located in Balboa Park, and he invited me to come down and run my trains on the club layout. One Sunday, I met him in Balboa Park and for the very first time I got to run my dad's 347C Santa Fe "Warbonnet" on the museum's big layout.

Right then and there, I decided to become a member of the San Diego Model Railroad Club. A fellow named Mike Thornhill took me around and introduced me to some of the club members who were there that day. I told several people about how I missed out buying a second Atlas 2357 switch engine, including one of my fellow club members, Gene Forbes.

A few months later, I was selected to be the keynote speaker at a National Model Railroad Association convention in San Diego. I ran the video of me riding my dad's red Santa Fe "Warbonnet" engine, which is on display at the beautiful Sacramento railroad museum.

After the video ran, I was in for the surprise of my life. Apparently, Gene was the one who had bought the second Atlas 2357 switch engine at Railmaster Hobbies not long after I had bought mine. After hearing my story he decided he wanted to give me the engine, so he worked it out with the guy who was running the banquet, Don Fowler, to present the engine to me on stage.

He did precisely that. Before I knew what was happening, he grabbed the microphone from me and said, "Shotgun, that 2357 engine you were looking for – I'm the guy who bought it, and I'd like to present it to you." Nothing like that had ever happened to me. I was totally blown away.

Another member of the San Diego Model Railroad Museum is Jerry Jackson, an expert in painting HO model trains. He makes plastic trains look greasy and dirty, and does the best graffiti by hand on the box cars. As soon as we met, Jerry said," Hey, I worked with your dad, John Irwin – I was your dad's brakeman on the Santa Fe."

It took a year, but finally it was time for Lloyd and Betsy Kluesner to start working on my layout. Jhani Kaye and I made many visits to Lloyd's workshop, where we saw my layout starting to come together.

Jhani had a wonderful idea: After we saw the layout starting to take shape and Lloyd and Betsy began to put the finishing touches on it, Jhani said, "Let's get the green screen so in post-production we can put clouds in it and make it look like a real city."

We started at 4 one Sunday afternoon. We asked four operators to run trains to get the shots Jhani wanted. We shot into the late night and then past midnight into the early

Watch a video of Shotgun Tom's model railroad layout filmed by Jhani Kaye.

morning hours. Lloyd looked like he was sleeping from an upright position as he was running the trains and positioning the green screen.

Around 3 a.m., I suggested to Jhani, "Shouldn't we pack up the trains and come back tomorrow?"

Jhani said, "No, I have two more scenes to shoot." We shot those two scenes and finally finished up at 7 a.m. Monday morning.

The next day, Jhani went to his studio and posted the video. He made the cars move around the layout and, using special effects, created fire in one of the buildings and another fire on top of another building.

For sound, we played the "Eyewitness News" theme and cut to a shot of a real anchorman, Harold Greene, talking about a fire in the city.

We wound up winning a national Telly Award for editing and production of "Shotgun Tom Kelly's HO Train Layout." Lloyd and Betsy have one of the awards proudly displayed in their workshop.

In model railroading, railroaders typically build their own layouts. I used to call myself a phony model railroader, because I had someone else build my layout, but one of my friends said, "No, don't call yourself a phony model railroader. You're a checkbook model railroader."

My friend Don Fowler – a retired commander with the San Diego Sheriff's Department – is also an avid model railroader.

Don is referred to as a Master Model Railroader (MMR). To get that distinction, you have to pass several projects sanctioned by the NMRA. His layout is N scale, smaller than my HO scale layout. Don got me to join the NMRA. It's a great organization with conventions all over the United States.

After Lloyd delivered the layout, I noticed a couple of empty spots where I could put in buildings on my own. I bought this building from Arnie's Trains that I thought would be the perfect addition! But when I got home, it turned out to be too big.

I panicked and told Don Fowler about my predicament. He told me not to worry. "We'll kit bash it," he said. He meant that we would carefully cut a chunk off the building before assembling it and then smoothen and paint it. It looks great on my layout! I was so happy with the way it turned out that Don helped me do that with another building.

So you see, I *can* do work on my own layout! Don tells me that working on my layout is proof of getting my hands dirty.

Since I brought my HO train layout home and installed it in my garage, so that it lifts up from my pool table, it has been featured on several television shows and newscasts. One appearance was on weatherman Dave Scott's "World of Wonder" on KUSI TV.

Watch a report on KUSI's Dave Scott's World of Wonder about Shotgun Tom's model railroad layout.

Model railroading is a really fun hobby for me. In a strange way I think I enjoy it so much because it keeps me in touch with the memory of dad. Even though he never wanted me to have a train set when I was a kid, I'm sure he'd be OK with it now. When I run my trains, I feel in touch with the spirit of my dad, John Irwin, the old Santa Fe railroad man.

Hollywood Media Professionals

During my last few years at KRTH I was approached by "Commander" Chuck Street, the traffic reporter on KIIS FM for many years. He asked me to join a group called the Pacific Pioneer Broadcasters.

They met on a monthly basis and their main purpose was to get together and socialize with other media professionals. I found it entertaining to have lunch and hang out with some of the radio and TV personalities I had always admired.

During each luncheon, a celebrity would be honored. It was so great to meet honorees such as my good friend Mike Love of the Beach Boys, Dick Cavett, Regis Philbin, Richard Chamberlain, Frankie Valli, Vin Scully, Carl Reiner, Art LaBoe, Tony Orlando, and Henry "The Fonz" Winkler.

When Henry introduced me to his friends in

attendance, he referred to me as one of his favorite radio personalities. That blew me away!

On March 27, 2015, I was presented with the Art Gilmore Career Achievement Award at the Pacific Pioneer Broadcasters luncheon at the Sportsmen's Lodge in Sherman Oaks, California.

A couple of years later I was elected president of the group. My duties included being the emcee of the luncheon. I thoroughly enjoyed that part of my presidency.

However, about a year into my term, the board became concerned about the membership. Hoping to attract younger members of the media – and thinking a rebrand was in order – they decided to change the name of the group to Hollywood Media Professionals.

Photo from Irwin Family Archives

John Stamos, Melanie Irwin,
Mike Love, Linda Irwin, Shotgun Tom.

A year after the name change had been implemented – and just as we were gaining momentum – what happens? COVID hit!

I can't stand it! All luncheons were canceled, and our board meetings were held via Zoom.

This definitely put a damper on our group, and it was never the same since. After my term ran out, I decided to withdraw from the organization.

Watch a video clip prepared for the Pacific Pioneer Broadcasters ceremony honoring Shotgun Tom with the Art Gilmore Career Achievement Award.

2023 California Music Award

In the early summer of 2023, I was contacted by Mike Copley, who informed me that I was to be inducted into the California Music Hall of Fame. It took me by complete surprise.

I was to receive my award along with: Rick Derringer, who was lead singer of the McCoys ("Hang on Sloopy") and the Edgar Winter Group and, later, a successful solo artist ("Rock 'n' Roll Hoochie Koo"); Chris Montez, who once headlined over the Beatles on the strength of his early Sixties hit "Let's Dance"; Ron Dante, lead singer of the Archies ("Sugar Sugar"); Cannibal and the Headhunters ("Land of 1,000 Dances"); Merilee Rush ("Angel of the Morning"); Chuck Negron of Three Dog Night; and several other recipients.

WOW! What a talented group of performers!

The awards presentation ceremony was held in Temecula at the Performing Arts Center, with

Wink Martindale as emcee. Along with being inducted into the Hall of Fame, Wink and I were also honored to receive the "B.J. Thomas Raindrops award."

It was presented to us by Gloria Thomas, widow of B.J. Thomas, whose "Raindrops Keep Fallin' On My Head" was one of the biggest Top 40 hits of 1969, made even bigger as the unforgettable anchor song of the soundtrack for *Butch Cassidy & The Sundance Kid*.

I asked my very dear friend, Jhani Kaye, to present me with the Hall of Fame Award. As always, Jhani's presentation was professional and smooth, sprinkled with a touch of humor.

I was also very pleased that so many of my friends were in attendance, along with several out-of-town SiriusXM 60s Gold channel channel listeners who had purchased tickets for the event. The awards ceremony was quite entertaining, because the inductees all performed their top hits. It turned out to be quite a day!

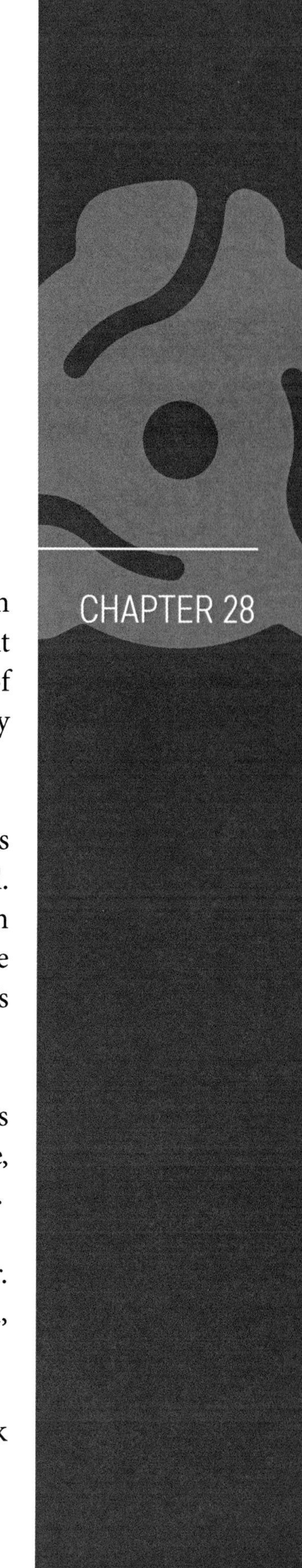

Signoff!

I sincerely want to thank you for hangin' in with me through this book. Before I go, I want to bring you up to date on myself and some of my nearest and dearest, the friends and family members you've met in these pages.

Let's start with Jack Vincent. Jack was with us for many years, for which I'll always be grateful. He never missed a pool hall night. Seated in his special chair in the center of the action, he would puff on a cigar, sip one of John Fewel's exotic tequilas and quietly take it all in.

He didn't speak that often, but when he did it was always direct and to the point. Sometimes wise, sometimes side-splittingly funny, sometimes both.

Jack always nailed it with the perfect capper. You'd almost forget he was there and then, boom! The perfect line, every time.

Eventually, he stopped driving, and I would pick

him up and take him home, which I didn't mind doing. He lived just 15 minutes from me, guaranteeing us a little private time, which I always looked forward to.

At the age of 98, Jack was hospitalized for a gallbladder blockage. The hospital wouldn't operate for fear that he would die on the operating table, so Jack was left with a blocked common bile duct that led to pancreatitis, a very painful condition.

Jack wanted to get out of the hospital and go back to his apartment. His wife, Nona, was gone, as were his brothers and sister. His only remaining relatives, nephew Scott Oatsdean and his family, and his niece, Sherry, lived in Kansas.

Scott was only able to visit from time to time, so he requested that we arrange for round-the-clock caregivers to look after Jack. My wife, Linda, and our good friend, radio engineer Bill Lipis, made certain to drop by his apartment each and every day to bring him supplies. I was still at KRTH, so I could only visit with him on the weekends.

Besides the three of us, Jack had several other friends who would visit during the week. Bill Martin would bring Jack the *National Enquirer* each week. Jack enjoyed reading that magazine cover to cover.

Jack stuck it out for another eight months, but in January 2016 he passed. He almost made it to 100. He meant so much to me. He was one of the first radio guys I met and the first to believe in me and encourage me to make my dream a reality. Sunny Jim Price and Don Howard were also mentors, but Jack was almost like a second father to me. Not a day goes by that I don't think of him.

Jack's memorial was at one of his favorite restaurants, Lido's in Lemon Grove. In the back room, we put up a rented big-screen TV. We showed a video of Jack doing a "Tonight Show" in my garage during his 90th birthday celebration. People said it was like having Jack alive at the party.

Everybody was very impressed with the touching video tribute to Jack that our good friend Art Vuolo had put together.

There wasn't a dry eye in the room!

We had an RCA 77 DX microphone set up so people could come up after the video and share a personal story about Jack.

That microphone was the same mic that Jack used during his all-night show in Santee on KCBQ. In the KCBQ monument video, we featured Jack reciting his sign-off as he did every morning when he threw it back to the KCBQ studio at 7th and Ash in downtown San Diego. "This is Jack Vincent here, saying so long, be good, drive carefully, have a pleasant day today and remember, a big smile costs you nothin.' So long, you."

So long, Jack.

Watch Jack Vincent's memorial.

I probably don't have to tell you how much my family means to me, and I'm happy to report that as of this writing, we're all doing well.

My daughter, Melanie, is a registered nurse. At her graduation, her professor came up to me and said, "Your daughter knows the information, but the most important thing that she has is that she is nurturing. That is a very important quality for a nurse to have."

Melanie is also an accomplished musician. She plays the piano beautifully. Once we were visiting Johnny Mathis at his home. Melanie sat down at Johnny's Steinway piano and played "Clocks" by Coldplay. Johnny was very impressed.

Melanie also enjoys playing guitar and always looks forward to when my brother-in-law, Richard Brockman, comes to town so they can have a regular "hootenanny," both playing their guitars and her piano.

Linda, Nick, my sister-in-law, Cissy, and I love listening to the two of them playing everything from rock to down-home blues.

Quite a hoot!

On a side note, we swiped an idea from Phlash Phelps (who does mornings on SiriusXM 60s Gold) and added a QR code to our Christmas cards for the past two years.

The first year, the code took you to a video of Melanie playing the song from the "Charlie Brown Christmas" cartoon on the piano while the three of us danced around. The following year (2023), Melanie played her guitar and sang Brenda Lee's "Rockin' Around the Christmas Tree."

Not sure what we'll do for our 2024 Christmas card; maybe Nick and Melanie will sing a duet. Who knows?

Photo from Irwin Family Archives

The Irwin family's 2023 Christmas card.

My son, Nick, retired as a Navy Chief Petty Officer after a 20-year career in IT on June 1, 2023. His retirement ceremony was held at North Island Naval Air Station in Coronado. The ceremony was very moving. I had the honor of being the

Watch the Irwin family's 2023 Christmas card come alive.

Photo from Irwin Family Archives

Proud father and son moment: Shotgun Tom with son Nick Irwin, newly retired as a Navy Chief Petty Officer.

emcee. Many of Nick's friends and family attended. After the ceremony, several of his Navy shipmates came up to me to say how Nick had inspired them in so many ways. They all said he was truly one of the best leaders they'd ever had.

My heart swelled with pride.

One year after his retirement from the Navy, Nick completed another milestone. With his family and friends in the audience at Chapman University in Orange, California, Nick proudly was hooded as he received his Ph.D. in Education. And to add to the excitement of the day as we all chanted "Dr. Nick, Dr. Nick", he was presented with two awards; the Outstanding Educator Award plus the Distinguished Doctoral Student Award.

While tirelessly researching and writing his dissertation, Nick was teaching classes at Chapman University. He is currently planning to work with the veterans community, to which he feels a great connection. He also loves the outdoors. Two of his passions are hiking and beach volleyball.

I've known my wife, Linda, since 1966, when we were both teenagers. As you'll recall, in 1970, when Linda was working at KCBQ in the traffic department and I was going to get demoted from KGB to a station in Fresno, it was Linda who stepped up and convinced Buzz Bennett and Rich Brother Robbin to bring me on board at KCBQ. That's when our good friendship blossomed into love.

Linda has guided me through many wonderful things in my life, and helped me make some very tough decisions. Without her I would not be where I am today.

She was a PTA president for many years when our children were enrolled in both elementary and high school. Currently, she is a member of the Del Cerro unit of Rady Children's Hospital Auxiliary. She's an avid reader and enjoys playing bridge. She still is employed at iHeart Radio, working part-time in the traffic department.

She is the love of my life and always will be.

Speaking of life, it threw me a bit of a curve in April 2014 while I was at K-Earth, still traveling back to San Diego on weekends. One Monday morning, before getting on the freeway for the 120-mile return trip to L.A., I went in to see my cardiologist, Dr. Kevin Rapeport. He gave me an EKG, took my blood pressure and it looked like everything was fine.

Then he asked me a question: "Do you have any pain in your chest? Actually, I did. When walking to work from my Park LaBrea apartment to K-Earth, I would feel some pressure building up in my chest. I would stop and it would go away. But when I continued my walk, pressure would build up again. I thought maybe I was just out of shape. But when Dr. Rapeport heard my story, he sent me downstairs to the nuclear cardiologists for a test. The test showed I had blockage in my heart.

The doctor rushed me to the Cath Lab. My daughter Melanie, who was on duty, took a look at my veins. Dr. Rapeport evaluated the information and delegated Melanie to break the news to me: "Daddy, you're going to have an operation." The decision was made to let me rest, spend the night in the hospital and have the operation the next day. I contacted K-Earth and asked them to arrange a fill-in.

The next morning, they rolled me into surgery. I met my anesthesiologist, Dr. Yuri Gelland, and my surgeon, Dr. Kumjian. So much blockage was found that I ended up needing a quadruple bypass!

I should have known something was up. Heart problems run in my family. My brothers, Greg and Bob, both dealt with heart problems. My mother had a heart problem and my dad died of a heart attack. I was lucky. They caught it in time. As I tell people, I did NOT have a heart attack! But I *was* a ticking time bomb. Had Dr. Rapeport not asked me that question about chest pain, I might not be writing this today.As I recovered, I wanted to go public with my experience so that maybe I could help other people who might have the same problem. So K-Earth worked out a deal with CBS 2 in Los Angeles to cover my progress. Some of my friends thought it was a publicity stunt. Some stunt!

After I got back to work, my good friend, then-City Councilman Tom LaBonge, welcomed me back on my first day back on the air with a city of Los Angeles proclamation. Ironically, he would die a few years later at 67 – of cardiac arrest.

The hospital at which I'd undergone my operation, Grossmont, decided that they wanted me to be the keynote speaker for a fundraiser gala to raise money for a new Cath Lab. At the gala, I felt like David Letterman introducing his doctors on television. They allowed me to bring all three of my doctors up on stage. It was really a great night.

With new veins in my heart, I feel I have a new lease on life, and I want to thank everybody who supported me – my doctors, my family, my friends and my wonderful listeners.

You can't go through a life-threatening situation like I did without confronting the mystery of mortality. The experience has made me appreciate my many blessings. My wonderful family, the many, many great friendships I've forged over the years and the great gift it's been to have a dream and be able to live it.

I couldn't be happier about being on the SiriusXM 60s Gold channel. It's the perfect place for me. I loved listening to that music in high school and then getting to play it on the air as a baby DJ, working my way back to San Diego through the smaller markets. It's the soundtrack of my youth and I never get tired of it. And I treasure the opportunity to share it with the SiriusXM listeners who love it as much as I do. I humbly thank SiriusXM and my wonderful listeners for giving me the opportunity.

From here on out, all I want to do is what I've always done, what I've wanted to do ever since I was a 10-year-old kid. I just wanna play the hits!!

Acknowledgements

I couldn't have written this book alone – and, in fact, I didn't.

I talked it.

Neil Ross, the legendary voice actor, did the actual writing after I sent him recordings of me talking about my life on my iPhone. Neil did a fabulous job and I owe him a tremendous debt of thanks. Then Thomas K. Arnold, the journalist, edited the book, polishing up our copy even more.

Thanks to my car buddy, C. Van Tune (former Editor-in-Chief of *Motor Trend Magazine*, and a popular ESPN TV host) for his extra editing work, and making sure I got all the car references correct.

I also need to thank the late Jim Bohannon, the great talk show host. Every time I'd see him at radio conventions, he'd corner me and say, "Shotgun, you need to write a book."

Well, Jim, I did – sort of.

But my biggest thanks go to my wife, Linda. Linda's known me since I was 16. We've been together since the very early days of my career, through thick and thin, as they say – and she has always been the very best partner I could ever have imagined or hoped for. Linda also kept me on track with this book, which might have been her most challenging job in all the years we've been married.

And, believe me, there have been challenges....

I also want to thank my kids, Melanie and Nick, who have truly made their father proud and grown up into remarkable adults despite their father's crazy career, which included many nights away from home as well as parties and gatherings in our home.

And then I need to thank all the folks who have been a part of my career, and who helped jog my memory so I could deliver at least a semi-coherent recollection of my life and times. Many of them are mentioned in this book. Some aren't. And for that, I apologize. Keep in mind I never said I was a writer...

All I wanna do is play the hits.

Music Surveys

KPRI

FM 106.5 SOUND OF STEREO

EASY LISTENING 40

MAY 13, 1968

1. Honey - Bobby Goldsboro
2. The Good, The Bad & The Ugly - Hugo Montenegro
3. Love Is Blue - Paul Mauriat
4. Unicorn - Irish Rogers
5. I Can't Believe I'm Losing You - Frank Sinatra
6. Soul Coaxing - Raymond LeFevre
7. Scarborough Fair - Simon and Garfunkel
8. Master Jack - Four Jacks and A Jill
9. Sherry Don't Go - Lettermen
10. Delilah Don't Go - Tom Jones
11. You've Still Got A Place In My Heart - Dean Martin
12. Lilli Marlene - Al Martino
13. Do You Know The Way To San Jose - Dionne Warwick
14. Take Good Care Of My Baby - Bobby Vinton
15. Cabaret - Herb Albert
16. Cab Driver - Mills Brothers
17. Gentle On My Mind - Patti Page
18. Loving You Has Made Me Bananas
19. I Found You - Frankie Laine
20. Yesterday I Heard The Rain - Tony Bennett
21. I Wanna Live - Glen Campbell
22. Kiss Me Goodbye - Petula Clark
23. We Can Fly/Up-Up and Away - Al Hirt
24. Lonely Is The Name - Sammy Davis Jr.
25. Little Green Apples - Roger Miller
26. Mrs. Robinson - Simon and Garfunkel
27. Faithfully - Margaret Whiting
28. Why Say Goodbye - Connie Francis
29. 100 Years - Nancy Sinatra
30. L. David Sloane - Michele Lee
31. Look Of Love - Sergio Mendes and Brasil '66'
32. Your Heart Is Free Just Like The Wind - Vikki Carr
33. Love In Every Room - Paul Mauriat
34. Goin Away - Fireballs
35. Soul Serenade - Willie Mitchell
36. Wind Song - Wes Montgomery
37. Till You Come Back - Marilyan Maye
38. Face It Girl, It's Over - Nancy Wilson
39. Slick - Herb Albert
40. Nothing To Lose - Vic Damone

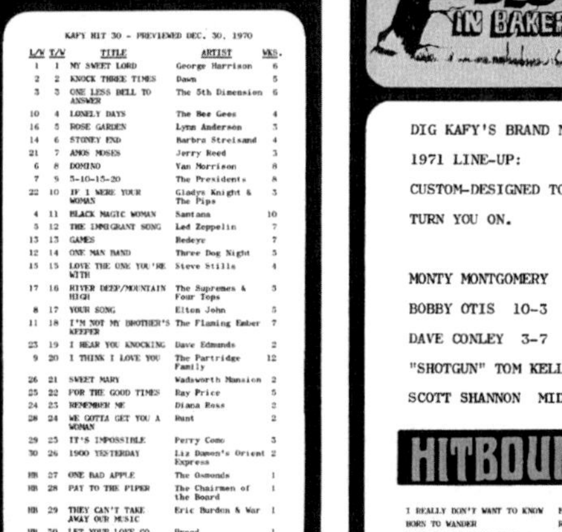

45's-Singles

KAFY HIT 30 - PREVIEWED DEC. 30, 1970

L/W	T/W	TITLE	ARTIST	WKS.
1	1	MY SWEET LORD	George Harrison	6
2	2	KNOCK THREE TIMES	Dawn	5
3	3	ONE LESS BELL TO ANSWER	The 5th Dimension	6
10	4	LONELY DAYS	The Bee Gees	4
16	5	ROSE GARDEN	Lynn Anderson	3
14	6	STONEY END	Barbra Streisand	4
21	7	AMOS MOSES	Jerry Reed	3
6	8	DOMINO	Van Morrison	8
7	9	5-10-15-20	The Presidents	8
22	10	IF I WERE YOUR WOMAN	Gladys Knight & The Pips	3
4	11	BLACK MAGIC WOMAN	Santana	10
5	12	THE IMMIGRANT SONG	Led Zeppelin	7
13	13	GAMES	Redeye	7
12	14	ONE MAN BAND	Three Dog Night	5
15	15	LOVE THE ONE YOU'RE WITH	Steve Stills	4
17	16	RIVER DEEP/MOUNTAIN HIGH	The Supremes & Four Tops	3
8	17	YOUR SONG	Elton John	5
11	18	I'M NOT MY BROTHER'S KEEPER	The Flaming Ember	7
23	19	I HEAR YOU KNOCKING	Dave Edmunds	2
9	20	I THINK I LOVE YOU	The Partridge Family	12
26	21	SWEET MARY	Wadsworth Mansion	2
25	22	FOR THE GOOD TIMES	Ray Price	5
24	23	REMEMBER ME	Diana Ross	2
28	24	WE GOTTA GET YOU A WOMAN	Runt	2
29	25	IT'S IMPOSSIBLE	Perry Como	3
30	26	1900 YESTERDAY	Liz Damon's Orient Express	2
HB	27	ONE BAD APPLE	The Osmonds	1
HB	28	PAY TO THE PIPER	The Chairmen of the Board	1
HB	29	THEY CAN'T TAKE AWAY OUR MUSIC	Eric Burdon & War	1
HB	30	LET YOUR LOVE GO	Bread	1

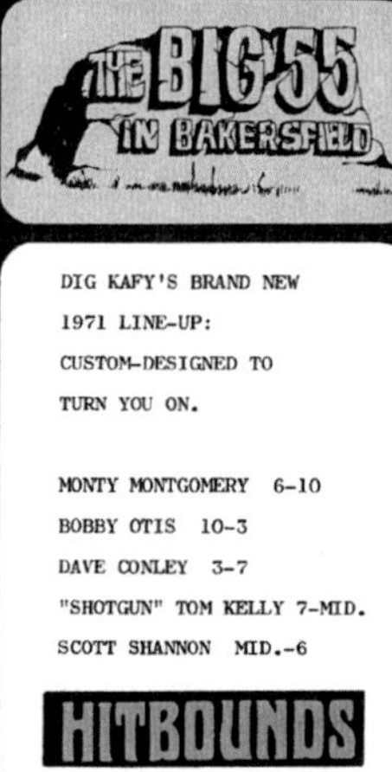

DIG KAFY'S BRAND NEW 1971 LINE-UP: CUSTOM-DESIGNED TO TURN YOU ON.

MONTY MONTGOMERY 6-10
BOBBY OTIS 10-3
DAVE CONLEY 3-7
"SHOTGUN" TOM KELLY 7-MID.
SCOTT SHANNON MID.-6

HITBOUNDS

I REALLY DON'T WANT TO KNOW	Elvis Presley
BORN TO WANDER	Rare Earth
WHEN I'M DEAD AND GONE	Bob Summers

Albums & Tapes

KAFY HEAVY ALBUMS - DEC. 30, 1970

L/W	T/W	TITLE	ARTIST
1	1	ALL THINGS MUST PASS	George Harrison
8	2	PENDULUM	Creedence Clearwater
4	3	LIVE ALBUM	Grand Funk Railroad
3	4	STEPHEN STILLS	Steve Stills
10	5	JOHN LENNON/PLASTIC ONO BAND	John Lennon & Plastic Ono Band
2	6	ABRAXAS	Santana
5	7	GREATEST HITS	Sly & The Family Stone
7	8	LED ZEPPELIN III	Led Zeppelin
6	9	ELTON JOHN	Elton John
19	10	AMERICAN BEAUTY ROSE	The Grateful Dead
13	11	TAP ROOT MANUSCRIPT	Neil Diamond
14	12	STEPPENWOLF 7	Steppenwolf
9	13	CLOSE TO YOU	Carpenters
20	14	THAT'S THE WAY IT IS	Elvis Presley
17	15	NATURALLY	Three Dog Night
22	16	JESUS CHRIST: SUPER-STAR	Soundtrack
23	17	WHALES AND NIGHTINGALES	Judy Collins
21	18	EMITT RHODES	Emitt Rhodes
24	19	WORST OF	Jefferson Airplane
16	20	SWEET BABY JAMES	James Taylor
-	21	BLOWS AGAINST THE EMPIRE	Paul Kantner
-	22	HIS BAND AND SWEET CHOIR	Van Morrison
25	23	UNCLE CHARLIE	Nitty Gritty Dirt Band
-	24	TO BE CONTINUED	Isaac Hayes
-	25	WATT	Ten Years After

The listing of records herein is the opinion of KAFY based on its survey of local sales, listener requests, and KAFY's judgment of the records appeal.

HIT BOUND

HEAVY MAKES YOU HAPPY/Staple Singers

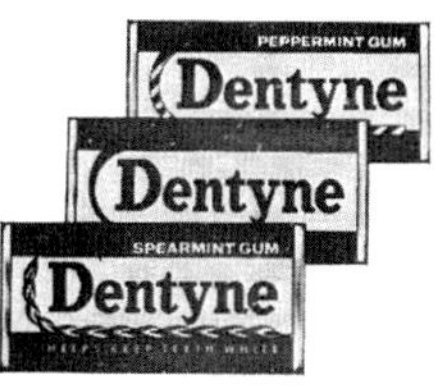

136/KGB

SAN DIEGO

OFFICIAL

ISSUE NO. 226
PREVIEWED FEBRUARY 22, 1971

The listing of records herein is the opinion of KGB based on its survey of record sales, listener requests, and KGB's judgment of the records' appeal.

KGB's "BOSS 30" RECORDS IN SAN DIEGO!

LAST WEEK	THIS WEEK	TITLE	ARTIST	LABEL	WEEKS ON BOSS 30
1	1	ONE BAD APPLE (3rd wk. #1)	Osmond Brothers	MGM	7
3	2	MR. BOJANGLES	Nitty Gritty Dirt Band	Liberty	5
4	3	AMOS MOSES	Jerry Reed	RCA	14
10	4	DOESN'T SOMEBODY WANT TO BE WANTED?	Partridge Family	Bell	5
2	5	KNOCK THREE TIMES	Dawn	Bell	11
5	6	FOR ALL WE KNOW	Carpenters	A & M	5
15	7	ME AND BOBBY MCGEE	Janis Joplin	Columbia	3
9	8	PROUD MARY	Ike & Tina Turner	Liberty	5
6	9	ROSE GARDEN	Lynn Anderson	Columbia	10
18	10	LOVE STORY	Francis Lai	U-A	2
7	11	IF YOU COULD READ MY MIND	Gordon Lightfoot	W.B.	4
11	12	MY SWEET LORD	George Harrison	Apple	15
8	13	WE GOTTA GET YOU A WOMAN	Runt	Ampex	9
12	14	MAMA'S PEARL	Jackson 5	Motown	5
21	15	HAVE YOU EVER SEEN THE RAIN	CCR	Fantasy	3
13	16	I HEAR YOU KNOCKIN'	Dave Edmunds	MAM(London)	6
20	17	WHAT IS LIFE	George Harrison	Apple	2
14	18	ONE LESS BELL TO ANSWER	5th Dimension	Bell	14
29	19	TEMPTATION EYES	Grassroots	ABC	2
17	20	ONE MAN BAND	3 Dog Night	Dunhill	12
16	21	LONELY DAYS	Bee Gees	Atco	10
30	22	SHE'S A LADY	Tom Jones	Parrot	2
HB	23	ANOTHER DAY	Paul McCartney	Apple	1
26	24	AMAZING GRACE	Judy Collins	Elektra	4
HB	25	SIT YOURSELF DOWN	Stephen Stills	Atlantic	1
23	26	I THINK I LOVE YOU	Partridge Family	Bell	21
19	27	SWEET MARY	Wadsworth Mansion	Sussex	8
HB	28	SOMEBODY'S WATCHING YOU	Little Sister	Stone Flower	1
HB	29	NO LOVE AT ALL	B.J. Thomas	Scepter	1
27	30	BLACK MAGIC WOMAN	Santana	Columbia	14

HIT BOUND

HIGH TIME WE WENT/Joe Cocker

136/KGB

SAN DIEGO

boss 30

136 KGB

OFFICIAL

ISSUE NO. 240
PREVIEWED MAY 31, 1971

The listing of records herein is the opinion of KGB based on its survey of record sales, listener requests, and KGB's judgment of the records' appeal.

KGB's "BOSS 30" RECORDS IN SAN DIEGO!

LAST WEEK	THIS WEEK	TITLE	ARTIST	LABEL	WEEKS ON BOSS 30
3	1	RAINY DAYS AND MONDAYS	Carpenters	A & M	6
1	2	SWEET AND INNOCENT	Donny Osmond	MGM	6
25	3	IT'S TOO LATE	Carole King	Ode	2
11	4	LOW DOWN	Chicago	Columbia	6
6	5	IT DON'T COME EASY	Ringo Starr	Apple	8
4	6	CHICK-A-BOOM	Daddy Dewdrop	Sunflower	10
7	7	WANT ADS	The Honey Cone	Hot Wax	4
12	8	TOAST AND MARMALADE	Tin Tin	Atco	4
10	9	BROWN SUGAR	Rolling Stones	Atlantic	6
20	10	INDIAN RESERVATION	Raiders	Columbia	2
17	11	SUPERSTAR	Murray Head	Decca	9
2	12	ME AND MY ARROW	Nilsson	RCA	9
13	13	LOVE HER MADLY	The Doors	Elektra	9
5	14	JOY TO THE WORLD	3 Dog Night	Dunhill	10
15	15	NEVER CAN SAY GOODBYE	Jackson 5	Motown	10
16	16	I LOVE YOU FOR ALL SEASONS	Fuzz	Calla	4
8	17	WOODSTOCK	Matthews Southern Comfort	Decca	5
9	18	PUT YOUR HAND IN THE HAND	Ocean	Kama Sutra	8
18	19	IF	Bread	Elektra	11
14	20	IT'S JUST MY IMAGINATION	Temptations	Gordy	13
19	21	ME AND YOU AND A DOG NAMED BOO	LOBO	Big Tree	11
HB	22	DOUBLE LOVIN'	The Osmonds	MGM	1
23	23	STAY AWHILE	The Bells	Polydor	8
22	24	RED-EYE BLUES	Redeye	Pentagram	5
21	25	WHEN YOU'RE HOT YOU'RE HOT	Jerry Reed	RCA	4
24	26	WHAT'S GOING ON	Marvin Gaye	Tamla	10
29	27	I AM....I SAID	Neil Diamond	Uni	12
28	28	ONE TOKE OVER THE LINE	Brewer & Shipley	Kama Sutra	15
HB	29	WHOLESALE LOVE	Buddy Miles	Mercury	1
HB	30	RINGS	Cymorron	Entrance	1

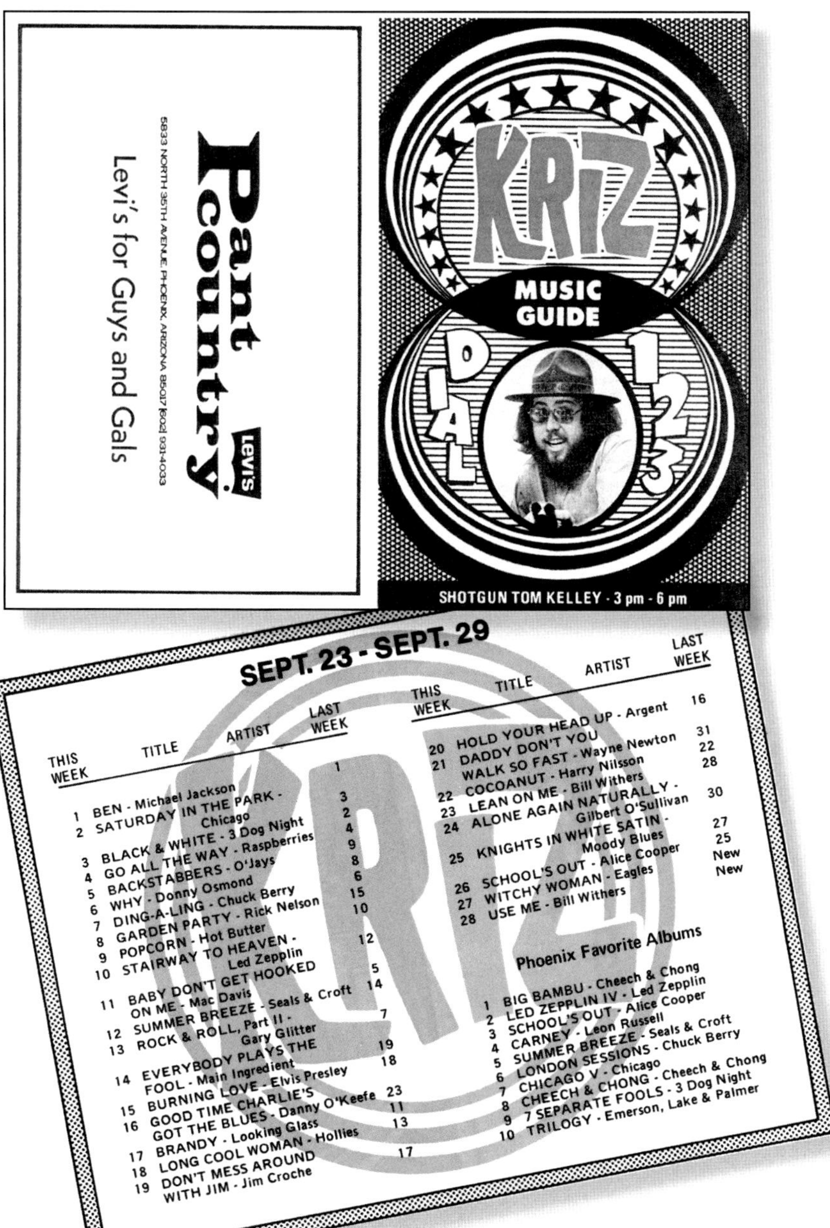

Pant Country
Levi's
5833 NORTH 35TH AVENUE, PHOENIX, ARIZONA 85017 (602) 931-4033
Levi's for Guys and Gals

KRIZ
MUSIC GUIDE
DIAL 1230
SHOTGUN TOM KELLEY · 3 pm - 6 pm

SEPT. 23 - SEPT. 29

THIS WEEK	TITLE - ARTIST	LAST WEEK
1	BEN - Michael Jackson	1
2	SATURDAY IN THE PARK - Chicago	3
3	BLACK & WHITE - 3 Dog Night	2
4	GO ALL THE WAY - Raspberries	4
5	BACKSTABBERS - O'Jays	9
6	WHY - Donny Osmond	8
7	DING-A-LING - Chuck Berry	6
8	GARDEN PARTY - Rick Nelson	15
9	POPCORN - Hot Butter	10
10	STAIRWAY TO HEAVEN - Led Zepplin	12
11	BABY DON'T GET HOOKED ON ME - Mac Davis	5
12	SUMMER BREEZE - Seals & Croft	14
13	ROCK & ROLL, Part II - Gary Glitter	7
14	EVERYBODY PLAYS THE FOOL - Main Ingredient	19
15	BURNING LOVE - Elvis Presley	18
16	GOOD TIME CHARLIE'S GOT THE BLUES - Danny O'Keefe	23
17	BRANDY - Looking Glass	11
18	LONG COOL WOMAN - Hollies	13
19	DON'T MESS AROUND WITH JIM - Jim Croche	17
20	HOLD YOUR HEAD UP - Argent	16
21	DADDY DON'T YOU WALK SO FAST - Wayne Newton	31
22	COCOANUT - Harry Nilsson	22
23	LEAN ON ME - Bill Withers	28
24	ALONE AGAIN NATURALLY - Gilbert O'Sullivan	30
25	KNIGHTS IN WHITE SATIN - Moody Blues	27
26	SCHOOL'S OUT - Alice Cooper	25
27	WITCHY WOMAN - Eagles	New
28	USE ME - Bill Withers	New

Phoenix Favorite Albums

1. BIG BAMBU - Cheech & Chong
2. LED ZEPPLIN IV - Led Zepplin
3. SCHOOL'S OUT - Alice Cooper
4. CARNEY - Leon Russell
5. SUMMER BREEZE - Seals & Croft
6. LONDON SESSIONS - Chuck Berry
7. CHICAGO V - Chicago
8. CHEECH & CHONG - Cheech & Chong
9. 7 SEPARATE FOOLS - 3 Dog Night
10. TRILOGY - Emerson, Lake & Palmer

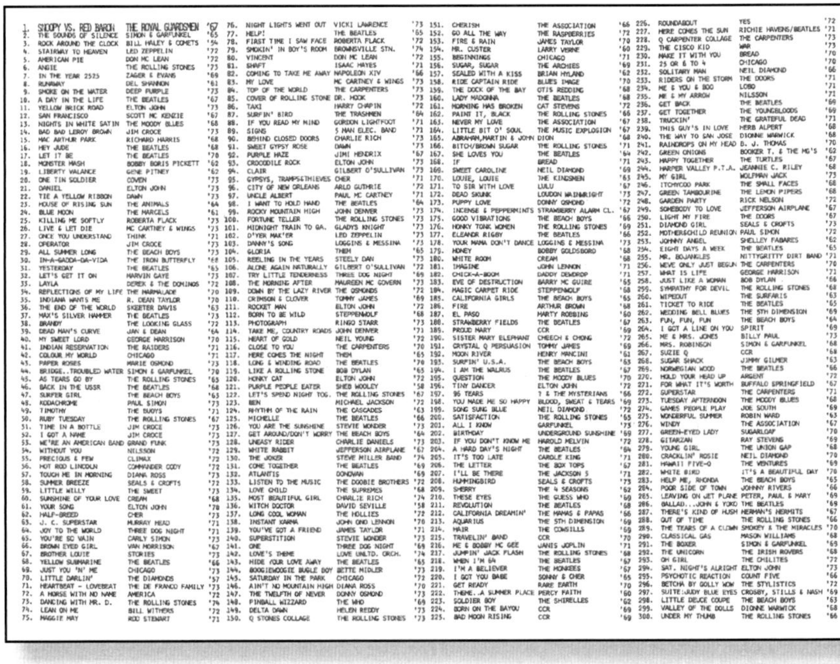

1.	SNOOPY VS. RED BARON	THE ROYAL GUARDSMEN	'67
2.	THE SOUNDS OF SILENCE	SIMON & GARFUNKEL	'65
3.	ROCK AROUND THE CLOCK	BILL HALEY & COMETS	'54
4.	STAIRWAY TO HEAVEN	LED ZEPPELIN	'72
5.	AMERICAN PIE	DON MC LEAN	'72
6.	ANGIE	THE ROLLING STONES	'73
7.	IN THE YEAR 2525	ZAGER & EVANS	'69
8.	RUNAWAY	DEL SHANNON	'61
9.	SMOKE ON THE WATER	DEEP PURPLE	'73
10.	A DAY IN THE LIFE	THE BEATLES	'67
11.	YELLOW BRICK ROAD	ELTON JOHN	'73
12.	SAN FRANCISCO	SCOTT MC KENZIE	'67
13.	NIGHTS IN WHITE SATIN	THE MOODY BLUES	'68
14.	BAD BAD LEROY BROWN	JIM CROCE	'73
15.	MAC ARTHUR PARK	RICHARD HARRIS	'68
16.	HEY JUDE	THE BEATLES	'68
17.	LET IT BE	THE BEATLES	'70
18.	MONSTER MASH	BOBBY BORIS PICKETT	'62
19.	LIBERTY VALANCE	GENE PITNEY	'62
20.	ONE TIN SOLDIER	COVEN	'73
21.	DANIEL	ELTON JOHN	'73
22.	TIE A YELLOW RIBBON	DAWN	'73
23.	HOUSE OF RISING SUN	THE ANIMALS	'64
24.	BLUE MOON	THE MARCELS	'61
25.	KILLING ME SOFTLY	ROBERTA FLACK	'73
26.	LIVE & LET DIE	MC CARTNEY & WINGS	'73
27.	ONCE YOU UNDERSTAND	THINK	'71
28.	OPERATOR	JIM CROCE	'73
29.	ALL SUMMER LONG	THE BEACH BOYS	'73
30.	IN-A-GADDA-DA-VIDA	THE IRON BUTTERFLY	'68
31.	YESTERDAY	THE BEATLES	'65
32.	LET'S GET IT ON	MARVIN GAYE	'73
33.	LAYLA	DEREK & THE DOMINOS	'72
34.	REFLECTIONS OF MY LIFE	THE MARMALADE	'70
35.	INDIANA WANTS ME	R. DEAN TAYLOR	'70
36.	THE END OF THE WORLD	SKEETER DAVIS	'63
37.	MAX'S SILVER HAMMER	THE BEATLES	'73
38.	BRANDY	THE LOOKING GLASS	'72
39.	DEAD MAN'S CURVE	JAN & DEAN	'64
40.	MY SWEET LORD	GEORGE HARRISON	'70
41.	INDIAN RESERVATION	THE RAIDERS	'71
42.	COLOUR MY WORLD	CHICAGO	'71
43.	PAPER ROSES	MARIE OSMOND	'73
44.	BRIDGE..TROUBLED WATER	SIMON & GARFUNKEL	'70
45.	AS TEARS GO BY	THE ROLLING STONES	'65
46.	BACK IN THE USSR	THE BEATLES	'68
47.	SURFER GIRL	THE BEACH BOYS	'63
48.	KODACHROME	PAUL SIMON	'73
49.	TIMOTHY	THE BUOYS	'71
50.	RUBY TUESDAY	THE ROLLING STONES	'67
51.	TIME IN A BOTTLE	JIM CROCE	'73
52.	I GOT A NAME	JIM CROCE	'73
53.	WE'RE AN AMERICAN BAND	GRAND FUNK	'73
54.	WITHOUT YOU	NILSSON	'72
55.	PRECIOUS & FEW	CLIMAX	'72
56.	HOT ROD LINCOLN	COMMANDER CODY	'72
57.	TOUCH ME IN MORNING	DIANA ROSS	'73
58.	SUMMER BREEZE	SEALS & CROFTS	'72
59.	LITTLE WILLY	THE SWEET	'73
60.	SUNSHINE OF YOUR LOVE	CREAM	'68
61.	YOUR SONG	ELTON JOHN	'70
62.	HALF-BREED	CHER	'73
63.	J. C. SUPERSTAR	MURRAY HEAD	'71
64.	JOY TO THE WORLD	THREE DOG NIGHT	'71
65.	YOU'RE SO VAIN	CARLY SIMON	'73
66.	BROWN EYED GIRL	VAN MORRISON	'67
67.	BROTHER LOUIE	STORIES	'73
68.	YELLOW SUBMARINE	THE BEATLES	'66
69.	JUST YOU 'N' ME	CHICAGO	'73
70.	LITTLE DARLIN'	THE DIAMONDS	'57
71.	HEARTBEAT - LOVEBEAT	THE DE FRANCO FAMILY	'73
72.	A HORSE WITH NO NAME	AMERICA	'72
73.	DANCING WITH MR. D.	THE ROLLING STONES	'74
74.	LEAN ON ME	BILL WITHERS	'72
75.	MAGGIE MAY	ROD STEWART	'71
76.	NIGHT LIGHTS WENT OUT	VICKI LAWRENCE	'73
77.	HELP!	THE BEATLES	'65
78.	FIRST TIME I SAW FACE	ROBERTA FLACK	'72
79.	SMOKIN' IN BOY'S ROOM	BROWNSVILLE STN.	'74
80.	VINCENT	DON MC LEAN	'72
81.	SHAFT	ISAAC HAYES	'71
82.	COMING TO TAKE ME AWAY	NAPOLEON XIV	'66
83.	MY LOVE	MC CARTNEY & WINGS	'73
84.	TOP OF THE WORLD	THE CARPENTERS	'73
85.	COVER OF ROLLING STONE	DR. HOOK	'73
86.	TAXI	HARRY CHAPIN	'72
87.	SURFIN' BIRD	THE TRASHMEN	'64
88.	IF YOU READ MY MIND	GORDON LIGHTFOOT	'71
89.	SIGNS	5 MAN ELEC. BAND	'71
90.	BEHIND CLOSED DOORS	CHARLIE RICH	'73
91.	SWEET GYPSY ROSE	DAWN	'73
92.	PURPLE HAZE	JIMI HENDRIX	'67
93.	CROCODILE ROCK	ELTON JOHN	'73
94.	CLAIR	GILBERT O'SULLIVAN	'73
95.	GYPSYS, TRAMPS&THIEVES	CHER	'71
96.	CITY OF NEW ORLEANS	ARLO GUTHRIE	'72
97.	UNCLE ALBERT	PAUL MC CARTNEY	'71
98.	I WANT TO HOLD HAND	THE BEATLES	'64
99.	ROCKY MOUNTAIN HIGH	JOHN DENVER	'73
100.	FORTUNE TELLER	THE ROLLING STONES	'73
101.	MIDNIGHT TRAIN TO GA.	GLADYS KNIGHT	'73
102.	D'YER MAK'ER	LED ZEPPELIN	'73
103.	DANNY'S SONG	LOGGINS & MESSINA	'73
104.	GLORIA	THEM	'65
105.	REELING IN THE YEARS	STEELY DAN	'73
106.	ALONE AGAIN NATURALLY	GILBERT O'SULLIVAN	'72
107.	TRY LITTLE TENDERNESS	THREE DOG NIGHT	'69
108.	THE MORNING AFTER	MAUREEN MC GOVERN	'73
109.	DOWN BY THE LAZY RIVER	THE OSMONDS	'72
110.	CRIMSON & CLOVER	TOMMY JAMES	'69
111.	ROCKET MAN	ELTON JOHN	'72
112.	BORN TO BE WILD	STEPPENWOLF	'68
113.	PHOTOGRAPH	RINGO STARR	'73
114.	TAKE ME, COUNTRY ROADS	JOHN DENVER	'71
115.	HEART OF GOLD	NEIL YOUNG	'72
116.	CLOSE TO YOU	THE CARPENTERS	'70
117.	HERE COMES THE NIGHT	THEM	'65
118.	LONG & WINDING ROAD	THE BEATLES	'70
119.	LIKE A ROLLING STONE	BOB DYLAN	'65
120.	HONKY CAT	ELTON JOHN	'72
121.	PURPLE PEOPLE EATER	SHEB WOOLEY	'58
122.	LET'S SPEND NIGHT TOG.	THE ROLLING STONES	'67
123.	BEN	MICHAEL JACKSON	'72
124.	RHYTHM OF THE RAIN	THE CASCADES	'63
125.	MICHELLE	THE BEATLES	'66
126.	YOU ARE THE SUNSHINE	STEVIE WONDER	'73
127.	GET AROUND/DON'T WORRY	THE BEACH BOYS	'64
128.	UNEASY RIDER	CHARLIE DANIELS	'73
129.	WHITE RABBIT	JEFFERSON AIRPLANE	'67
130.	THE JOKER	STEVE MILLER BAND	'74
131.	COME TOGETHER	THE BEATLES	'69
132.	ATLANTIS	DONOVAN	'69
133.	LISTEN TO THE MUSIC	THE DOOBIE BROTHERS	'72
134.	LOVE CHILD	THE SUPREMES	'68
135.	MOST BEAUTIFUL GIRL	CHARLIE RICH	'74
136.	WITCH DOCTOR	DAVID SEVILLE	'58
137.	LONG COOL WOMAN	THE HOLLIES	'72
138.	INSTANT KARMA	JOHN ONO LENNON	'70
139.	YOU'VE GOT A FRIEND	JAMES TAYLOR	'71
140.	SUPERSTITION	STEVIE WONDER	'73
141.	ONE	THREE DOG NIGHT	'69
142.	LOVE'S THEME	LOVE UNLTD. ORCH.	'74
143.	HIDE YOUR LOVE AWAY	THE BEATLES	'65
144.	BOOGIEWOOGIE BUGLE BOY	BETTE MIDLER	'73
145.	SATURDAY IN THE PARK	CHICAGO	'72
146.	AIN'T NO MOUNTAIN HIGH	DIANA ROSS	'70
147.	THE TWELFTH OF NEVER	DONNY OSMOND	'73
148.	PINBALL WIZZARD	THE WHO	'69
149.	DELTA DAWN	HELEN REDDY	'73
150.	Q STONES COLLAGE	THE ROLLING STONES	'73
151.	CHERISH	THE ASSOCIATION	'66
152.	GO ALL THE WAY	THE RASPBERRIES	'72
153.	FIRE & RAIN	JAMES TAYLOR	'70
154.	MR. CUSTER	LARRY VERNE	'60
155.	BEGINNINGS	CHICAGO	'71
156.	SUGAR, SUGAR	THE ARCHIES	'69
157.	SEALED WITH A KISS	BRIAN HYLAND	'62
158.	RIDE CAPTAIN RIDE	BLUES IMAGE	'70
159.	THE DOCK OF THE BAY	OTIS REDDING	'68
160.	LADY MADONNA	THE BEATLES	'68
161.	MORNING HAS BROKEN	CAT STEVENS	'72
162.	PAINT IT, BLACK	THE ROLLING STONES	'66
163.	NEVER MY LOVE	THE ASSOCIATION	'67
164.	LITTLE BIT O' SOUL	THE MUSIC EXPLOSION	'67
165.	ABRAHAM,MARTIN & JOHN	DION	'68
166.	BITCH/BROWN SUGAR	THE ROLLING STONES	'71
167.	SHE LOVES YOU	THE BEATLES	'64
168.	IF	BREAD	'71
169.	SWEET CAROLINE	NEIL DIAMOND	'69
170.	LOUIE, LOUIE	THE KINGSMEN	'63
171.	TO SIR WITH LOVE	LULU	'67
172.	DEAD SKUNK	LOUDON WAINWRIGHT	'73
173.	PUPPY LOVE	DONNY OSMOND	'72
174.	INCENSE & PEPPERMINTS	STRAWBERRY ALARM CL.	'67
175.	GOOD VIBRATIONS	THE BEACH BOYS	'66
176.	HONKY TONK WOMEN	THE ROLLING STONES	'69
177.	ELEANOR RIGBY	THE BEATLES	'66
178.	YOUR MAMA DON'T DANCE	LOGGINS & MESSINA	'73
179.	HONEY	BOBBY GOLDSBORO	'68
180.	WHITE ROOM	CREAM	'68
181.	IMAGINE	JOHN LENNON	'71
182.	CHICK-A-BOOM	DADDY DEWDROP	'71
183.	EVE OF DESTRUCTION	BARRY MC GUIRE	'65
184.	MAGIC CARPET RIDE	STEPPENWOLF	'68
185.	CALIFORNIA GIRLS	THE BEACH BOYS	'65
186.	FIRE	ARTHUR BROWN	'68
187.	EL PASO	MARTY ROBBINS	'60
188.	STRAWBERRY FIELDS	THE BEATLES	'67
189.	PROUD MARY	CCR	'69
190.	SISTER MARY ELEPHANT	CHEECH & CHONG	'72
191.	CRYSTAL Q PERSUASION	TOMMY JAMES	'69
192.	MOON RIVER	HENRY MANCINI	'61
193.	SURFIN' U.S.A.	THE BEACH BOYS	'63
194.	I AM THE WALRUS	THE BEATLES	'67
195.	QUESTION	THE MOODY BLUES	'70
196.	TINY DANCER	ELTON JOHN	'72
197.	96 TEARS	? & THE MYSTERIANS	'66
198.	YOU MADE ME SO HAPPY	BLOOD, SWEAT & TEARS	'69
199.	SONG SUNG BLUE	NEIL DIAMOND	'72
200.	SATISFACTION	THE ROLLING STONES	'65
201.	ALL I KNOW	GARFUNKEL	'73
202.	BIRTHDAY	UNDERGROUND SUNSHINE	'69
203.	IF YOU DON'T KNOW ME	HAROLD MELVIN	'72
204.	A HARD DAY'S NIGHT	THE BEATLES	'64
205.	IT'S TOO LATE	CAROLE KING	'71
206.	THE LETTER	THE BOX TOPS	'67
207.	I'LL BE THERE	THE JACKSON 5	'71
208.	HUMMINGBIRD	SEALS & CROFTS	'73
209.	SHERRY	THE 4 SEASONS	'62
210.	THESE EYES	THE GUESS WHO	'69
211.	REVOLUTION	THE BEATLES	'68
212.	CALIFORNIA DREAMIN'	THE MAMAS & PAPAS	'66
213.	AQUARIUS	THE 5TH DIMENSION	'69
214.	HAIR	THE COWSILLS	'69
215.	TRAVELIN' BAND	CCR	'70
216.	ME & BOBBY MC GEE	JANIS JOPLIN	'71
217.	JUMPIN' JACK FLASH	THE ROLLING STONES	'68
218.	WHEN I'M 64	THE BEATLES	'67
219.	I'M A BELIEVER	THE MONKEES	'67
220.	I GOT YOU BABE	SONNY & CHER	'65
221.	GET READY	RARE EARTH	'70
222.	THEME..A SUMMER PLACE	PERCY FAITH	'60
223.	SOLDIER BOY	THE SHIRELLES	'62
224.	BORN ON THE BAYOU	CCR	'69
225.	BAD MOON RISING	CCR	'69
226.	ROUNDABOUT	YES	'72
227.	HERE COMES THE SUN	RICHIE HAVENS/BEATLES	'71
228.	Q CARPENTER COLLAGE	THE CARPENTERS	'73
229.	THE CISCO KID	WAR	'73
230.	MAKE IT WITH YOU	BREAD	'70
231.	25 OR 6 TO 4	CHICAGO	'70
232.	SOLITARY MAN	NEIL DIAMOND	'66
233.	RIDERS ON THE STORM	THE DOORS	'71
234.	ME & YOU & BOO	LOBO	'71
235.	ME & MY ARROW	NILSSON	'71
236.	GET BACK	THE BEATLES	'69
237.	GET TOGETHER	THE YOUNGBLOODS	'69
238.	TRUCKIN'	THE GRATEFUL DEAD	'71
239.	THIS GUY'S IN LOVE	HERB ALPERT	'68
240.	THE WAY TO SAN JOSE	DIONNE WARWICK	'68
241.	RAINDROPS ON MY HEAD	B. J. THOMAS	'70
242.	GREEN ONIONS	BOOKER T. & THE MG'S	'62
243.	HAPPY TOGETHER	THE TURTLES	'67
244.	HARPER VALLEY P.T.A.	JEANNIE C. RILEY	'68
245.	MY GIRL	WOLFMAN JACK	'73
246.	ITCHYCOO PARK	THE SMALL FACES	'68
247.	GREEN TAMBOURINE	THE LEMON PIPERS	'68
248.	GARDEN PARTY	RICK NELSON	'72
249.	SOMEBODY TO LOVE	JEFFERSON AIRPLANE	'67
250.	LIGHT MY FIRE	THE DOORS	'67
251.	DIAMOND GIRL	SEALS & CROFTS	'73
252.	MOTHER&CHILD REUNION	PAUL SIMON	'72
253.	JOHNNY ANGEL	SHELLEY FABARES	'62
254.	EIGHT DAYS A WEEK	THE BEATLES	'65
255.	MR. BOJANGLES	NITTYGRITTY DIRT BAND	'71
256.	WEVE ONLY JUST BEGUN	THE CARPENTERS	'70
257.	WHAT IS LIFE	GEORGE HARRISON	'71
258.	JUST LIKE A WOMAN	BOB DYLAN	'66
259.	SYMPATHY FOR DEVIL	THE ROLLING STONES	'68
260.	WIPEOUT	THE SURFARIS	'63
261.	TICKET TO RIDE	THE BEATLES	'65
262.	WEDDING BELL BLUES	THE 5TH DIMENSION	'69
263.	FUN, FUN, FUN	THE BEACH BOYS	'64
264.	I GOT A LINE ON YOU	SPIRIT	'69
265.	ME & MRS. JONES	BILLY PAUL	'73
266.	MRS. ROBINSON	SIMON & GARFUNKEL	'68
267.	SUZIE Q	CCR	'68
268.	SUGAR SHACK	JIMMY GILMER	'63
269.	NORWEGIAN WOOD	THE BEATLES	'66
270.	HOLD YOUR HEAD UP	ARGENT	'72
271.	FOR WHAT IT'S WORTH	BUFFALO SPRINGFIELD	'67
272.	SUPERSTAR	THE CARPENTERS	'71
273.	TUESDAY AFTERNOON	THE MOODY BLUES	'68
274.	GAMES PEOPLE PLAY	JOE SOUTH	'69
275.	WONDERFUL SUMMER	ROBIN WARD	'63
276.	WINDY	THE ASSOCIATION	'67
277.	GREEN-EYED LADY	SUGARLOAF	'70
278.	GITARZAN	RAY STEVENS	'69
279.	YOUNG GIRL	THE UNION GAP	'68
280.	CRACKLIN' ROSIE	NEIL DIAMOND	'70
281.	HAWAII FIVE-O	THE VENTURES	'69
282.	WHITE BIRD	IT'S A BEAUTIFUL DAY	'70
283.	HELP ME, RHONDA	THE BEACH BOYS	'65
284.	POOR SIDE OF TOWN	JOHNNY RIVERS	'66
285.	LEAVING ON JET PLANE	PETER, PAUL & MARY	'69
286.	BALLAD...JOHN & YOKO	THE BEATLES	'69
287.	THERE'S KIND OF HUSH	HERMAN'S HERMITS	'67
288.	OUT OF TIME	THE ROLLING STONES	'66
289.	THE TEARS OF A CLOWN	SMOKEY & THE MIRACLES	'70
290.	CLASSICAL GAS	MASON WILLIAMS	'68
291.	THE BOXER	SIMON & GARFUNKEL	'69
292.	THE UNICORN	THE IRISH ROVERS	'68
293.	OH GIRL	THE CHILITES	'72
294.	SAT. NIGHT'S ALRIGHT	ELTON JOHN	'73
295.	PSYCHOTIC REACTION	COUNT FIVE	'66
296.	BETCHA BY GOLLY WOW	THE STYLISTICS	'72
297.	SUITE:JUDY BLUE EYES	CROSBY, STILLS & NASH	'69
298.	LITTLE DEUCE COUPE	THE BEACH BOYS	'63
299.	VALLEY OF THE DOLLS	DIONNE WARWICK	'68
300.	UNDER MY THUMB	THE ROLLING STONES	'66

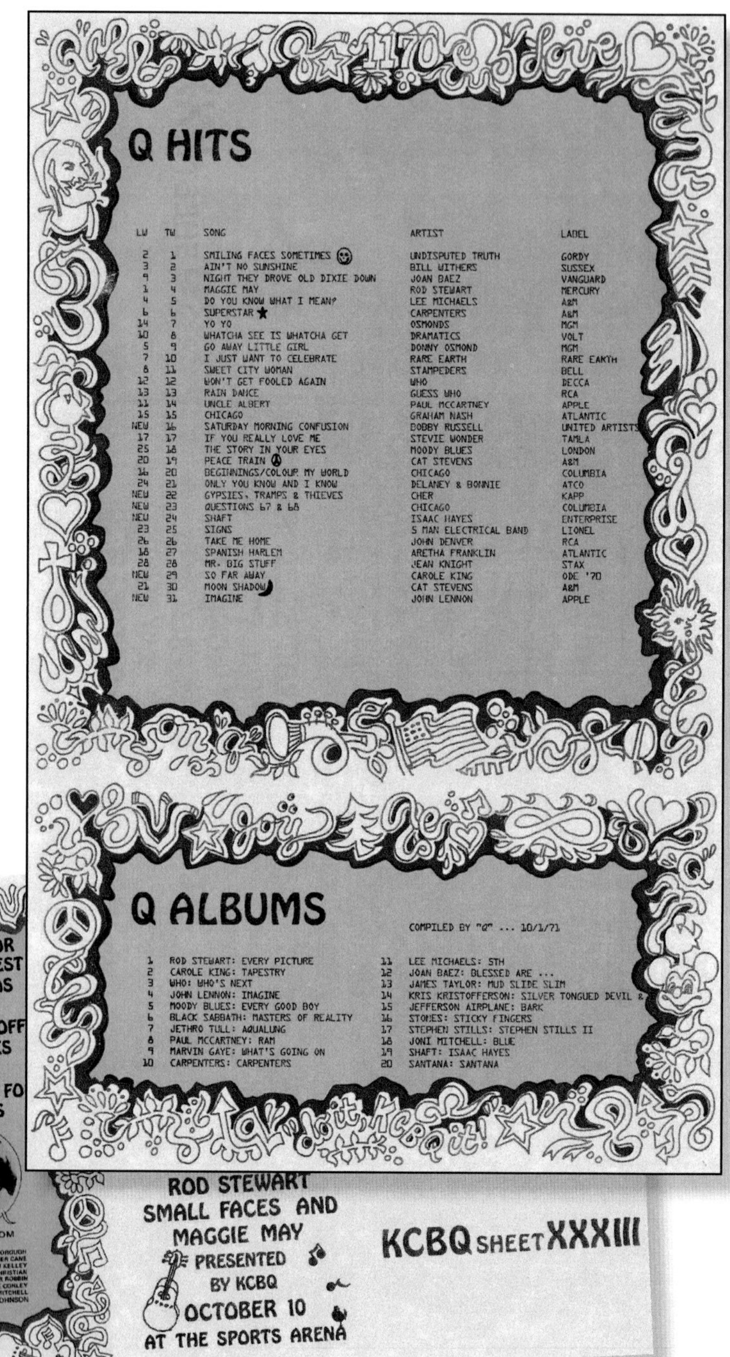

Q HITS

LW	TW	SONG	ARTIST	LABEL
2	1	SMILING FACES SOMETIMES	UNDISPUTED TRUTH	GORDY
3	2	AIN'T NO SUNSHINE	BILL WITHERS	SUSSEX
9	3	NIGHT THEY DROVE OLD DIXIE DOWN	JOAN BAEZ	VANGUARD
1	4	MAGGIE MAY	ROD STEWART	MERCURY
4	5	DO YOU KNOW WHAT I MEAN?	LEE MICHAELS	A&M
6	6	SUPERSTAR	CARPENTERS	A&M
14	7	YO YO	OSMONDS	MGM
10	8	WHATCHA SEE IS WHATCHA GET	DRAMATICS	VOLT
5	9	GO AWAY LITTLE GIRL	DONNY OSMOND	MGM
7	10	I JUST WANT TO CELEBRATE	RARE EARTH	RARE EARTH
8	11	SWEET CITY WOMAN	STAMPEDERS	BELL
12	12	WON'T GET FOOLED AGAIN	WHO	DECCA
13	13	RAIN DANCE	GUESS WHO	RCA
11	14	UNCLE ALBERT	PAUL MCCARTNEY	APPLE
15	15	CHICAGO	GRAHAM NASH	ATLANTIC
NEW	16	SATURDAY MORNING CONFUSION	BOBBY RUSSELL	UNITED ARTISTS
17	17	IF YOU REALLY LOVE ME	STEVIE WONDER	TAMLA
25	18	THE STORY IN YOUR EYES	MOODY BLUES	LONDON
20	19	PEACE TRAIN	CAT STEVENS	A&M
16	20	BEGINNINGS/COLOUR MY WORLD	CHICAGO	COLUMBIA
24	21	ONLY YOU KNOW AND I KNOW	DELANEY & BONNIE	ATCO
NEW	22	GYPSIES, TRAMPS & THIEVES	CHER	KAPP
NEW	23	QUESTIONS 67 & 68	CHICAGO	COLUMBIA
NEW	24	SHAFT	ISAAC HAYES	ENTERPRISE
23	25	SIGNS	5 MAN ELECTRICAL BAND	LIONEL
26	26	TAKE ME HOME	JOHN DENVER	RCA
18	27	SPANISH HARLEM	ARETHA FRANKLIN	ATLANTIC
28	28	MR. BIG STUFF	JEAN KNIGHT	STAX
NEW	29	SO FAR AWAY	CAROLE KING	ODE '70
21	30	MOON SHADOW	CAT STEVENS	A&M
NEW	31	IMAGINE	JOHN LENNON	APPLE

Q ALBUMS

COMPILED BY "Q" ... 10/1/71

1. ROD STEWART: EVERY PICTURE
2. CAROLE KING: TAPESTRY
3. WHO: WHO'S NEXT
4. JOHN LENNON: IMAGINE
5. MOODY BLUES: EVERY GOOD BOY
6. BLACK SABBATH: MASTERS OF REALITY
7. JETHRO TULL: AQUALUNG
8. PAUL MCCARTNEY: RAM
9. MARVIN GAYE: WHAT'S GOING ON
10. CARPENTERS: CARPENTERS
11. LEE MICHAELS: 5TH
12. JOAN BAEZ: BLESSED ARE ...
13. JAMES TAYLOR: MUD SLIDE SLIM
14. KRIS KRISTOFFERSON: SILVER TONGUED DEVIL &
15. JEFFERSON AIRPLANE: BARK
16. STONES: STICKY FINGERS
17. STEPHEN STILLS: STEPHEN STILLS II
18. JONI MITCHELL: BLUE
19. SHAFT: ISAAC HAYES
20. SANTANA: SANTANA

Q-Tips

GET SET FOR YOUR BIGGEST WIN YET AS KCBQ's GREAT RIP-OFF CONTINUES

QUICK TURN ON Q FO[R] DETAILS

SHOTGUN TOM

6 to 9. . . . HARRY SCARBOROUGH
9 to noon. . . . CHRISTOPHER CANE
noon to 3. SHOTGUN TOM KELLEY
3 to 6. . . . THE MAGIC CHRISTIAN
6 to 9. . . . RICH BROTHER ROBBIN
9 to midnight. . . . DAVE CONLEY
midnight to 6. . . LENNY MITCHELL
weekends. . . . BAT JOHNSON

ROD STEWART SMALL FACES AND MAGGIE MAY PRESENTED BY KCBQ OCTOBER 10 AT THE SPORTS ARENA

KCBQ SHEET XXXIII

HITS

THE TOP SELLING SONGS IN SAN DIEGO

WAS	IS	TITLE	ARTIST	WKS
1	1	JIVE TALKIN'	BEE GEES	7
2	2	THE HUSTLE	VAN McCOY	11
6	3	GET DOWN TONIGHT	KCBQ SUNSHINE BAND	4
3	4	WHY CAN'T WE BE FRIENDS	WAR	10
4	5	AT 17	JANIS IAN	7
9	6	FALLIN' IN LOVE	HAM.,J.F. & REY.	5
5	7	HOW SWEET IT IS	JAMES TAYLOR	7
16	8	MIRACLES	J STARSHIP	4
7	9	ONE OF THESE NIGHTS	EAGLES	12
17	10	FEELINGS	MORRIS ALBERT	4
10	11	LOVE WILL KEEP US	CPT & TENNILLE	15
20	12	FAME	DAVID BOWIE	2
14	13	RUN JOEY RUN	DAVID GEDDES	5
11	14	SOMEONE SAVED MY LIFE	ELTON	15
8	15	TUSH	ZZ TOP	6
12	16	I'M NOT IN LOVE	10 CC	12
13	17	THE WAY OF THE WORLD	EWF	5
QQ	18	THERE GOES ANOTHER LOVE SONG	OUTLAWS	1
X-TRA		MR. JAWS	STATION CREATION	
X-TRA		BAD BLOOD	ELTON & NEIL SEDAKA	

FAME (BOWIE/LENON/ALOMAR)

Fame—Makes a man take things over
Lets him loose and hard to swallow
Puts you there, where things are hollow.
Fame
Fame—Its mine—its mine—is just his line
To bind your time—it drives you to crime
Fame—What you like is in the limo
What you get is no tomorrow
What you need you have to borrow
Fame—Its not your brain—its just up the flame
That burns your change to keep you insane
Is it any wonder—I reject you first
Fame—fame—fame—fame
Is it any wonder—you're to cool to fool
Bully for you, chilly for me
Got to get a rain check on
pain

ALBUMS

WAS	IS	TITLE	ARTIST
1	1	ONE OF THESE NIGHTS	EAGLES
2	2	RED OCTUPUS	J STASHIP
7	3	CPT FANTASTIC	ELTON
4	4	GORILLA	JAMES TAYLOR
13	5	GOOD VIBRATIONS	BEACH BOYS
6	6	FANDANGO	ZZ TOP
3	7	CUT THE CAKE	AWB
12	8	FLEETWOOD MAC	FLEETWOOD MAC
5	9	BETWEEN THE LINES	JANIS IAN
9	10	OUTLAWS	OUTLAWS
8	11	WHY CAN'T WE BE FRIENDS	WAR
14	12	VENUS AND MARS	WINGS
QQ	13	KCBQ & SUNSHINE BAND	KCBQ SUNSHINE BAND
QQ	14	ATLANTIC CROSSING	ROD STEWART
15	15	HONEY	OHIO PLAYERS

HITS

WAS	IS	TITLE	ARTIST	WKS
1	1	CONVOY	CW MCCALL	4
2	2	50 WAYS TO LEAVE YOUR	PAUL SIMON	9
3	3	FLY ROBIN FLY	SILVER CONVENTION	13
4	4	LOVE ROLLER COASTER	OHIO PLAYERS	12
6	5	I WRITE THE SONGS	BARRY MANILOW	4
7	6	MAHOGANY	DIANA ROSS	5
5	7	LETS DO IT AGAIN	STAPLE SINGERS	8
9	8	EVIL WOMAN	ELO	4
15	9	YOU SEXY THING	HOT CHOCOLATE	3
14	10	FOX ON THE RUN	THE SWEET	6
11	11	18 WITH A BULLET	PETE WINGFIELD	7
12	12	SATURDAY NIGHT	BAY CITY ROLLERS	8
8	13	OVER MY HEAD	FLEETWOOD MAC	6
10	14	SING A SONG	EWF	4
16	15	FLY AWAY	JOHN DENVER	3
13	16	I LOVE MUSIC	O'JAYS	6
QQ	17	BREAKING UP IS HARD TO DO	NEIL SEDAKA	1
QQ	18	LOVE TO LOVE YOU BABY	DONNA SUMMER	1
QQ	19	BULLET	ELTON JOHN	1
QQ	20	THE WHITE KNIGHT	CLEDUS MAGGARD	2

COMPILED BY Q FOR JANUARY 19, 1976

OFFICIAL NATIONAL CB 10-CODE

10-1	RECEIVING POORLY
10-2	RECEIVING WELL
10-3	STOP TRANSMITTING
10-4	OK, MESSAGE RECEIVED
10-5	RELAY MESSAGE
10-6	BUSY, STAND BY
10-7	OUT OF SERVICE, LEAVING AIR
10-8	IN SERVICE, SUBJECT TO CALL
10-9	REPEAT MESSAGE
10-10	TRANSMISSION OVER, STANDING BY
10-11	TALKING TOO RAPIDLY
10-12	VISITORS PRESENT
10-13	ADVISE WEATHER/RD. CONDITIONS
10-16	MAKE PICKUP AT
10-17	URGENT BUSINESS
10-18	ANYTHING FOR US?
10-19	NOTHING FOR YOU, RETURN TO BASE
10-20	MY LOCATION IS ______
10-21	CALL BY TELEPHONE
10-22	REPORT IS PERSON TO ______
10-23	STAND BY
10-24	COMPLETED LAST ASSIGNMENT
10-25	CAN YOU CONTACT ______
10-26	DISREGARD LAST INFORMATION
10-27	I AM MOVING TO CHANNEL ______
10-28	IDENTIFY YOUR CHANNEL
10-29	TIME IS UP FOR CONTACT
10-30	DOES NOT CONFORM TO FCC RULES
10-32	I WILL GIVE YOU A RADIO CHECK
10-33	EMERGENCY TRAFFIC AT THIS STATION
10-34	TROUBLE AT THIS STATION, HELP NEEDED
10-35	CONFIDENTIAL INFORMATION
10-36	CORRECT TIME IS ______
10-37	WRECKER NEEDED AT ______
10-38	AMBULANCE NEEDED AT ______
10-39	YOUR MESSAGE DELIVERED
10-41	PLEASE TUNE TO CHANNEL ______
10-42	TRAFFIC ACCIDENT AT ______
10-43	TRAFFIC TIEUP AT ______
10-44	I HAVE A MESSAGE FOR YOU
10-45	ALL UNITS WITHIN RANGE PLEASE REPORT
10-50	BREAK CHANNEL ______
10-60	WHAT IS THE NEXT MESSAGE NUMBER?
10-62	UNABLE TO COPY, USE PHONE
10-63	NET DIRECTED TO ______
10-64	NET CLEAR
10-65	AWAITING NEXT MESSAGE/ASSIGNMENT
10-67	ALL UNITS COMPLY
10-70	FIRE AT ______
10-71	PROCEED WITH TRANSMISSION IN SEQUENCE
10-73	SPEED TRAP AT ______
10-75	YOU ARE CAUSING INTERFERENCE
10-77	NEGATIVE CONTACT
10-81	RESERVE ROOM FOR
10-84	MY TELEPHONE NUMBER IS ______
10-85	MY ADDRESS IS ______
10-89	RADIO REPAIRMAN NEEDED AT ______
10-90	I HAVE TVI
10-91	TALK CLOSER TO MIKE
10-92	YOUR TRANSMITTER IS OUT OF ADJUSTMENT
10-93	CHECK MY FREQUENCY ON THIS CHANNEL
10-94	PLEASE GIVE ME A LONG COUNT
10-95	TRANSMIT DEAD CARRIER FOR 5 SECONDS
10-99	MISSION COMPLETED, ALL UNITS SECURE
10-200	POLICE NEEDED AT ______

ALBUMS

1	1	STILL CRAZY	PAUL SIMON
3	2	HISSING OF SUMMER LAWNS	JONI MITCHELL
7	3	AMERICA HISTORY	AMERICA
8	4	ROCK OF THE WESTIES	ELTON
2	5	GRATITUDE	EWF
5	6	CHICAGOS GREATEST	CHICAGO
4	7	FLEETWOOD MAC	FLEETWOOD MAC
9	8	WIND ON THE WATER	CROSBY & NASH
12	10	BREAKAWAY	ART GARFUNKLE
QQ	11	DESIRE	BOB DYLAN
6	12	WISH YOU WERE HERE	PINK FLOYD
13	13	KCBQ SUNSHINE BAND	KCBQ SUNSHINE BAND
17	14	HONEY	OHIO PLAYERS
14	15	RED OCTOPUS	STARSHIP
QQ	16	NUMBERS	CAT STEVENS
10	17	FACE THE MUSIC	ELO
16	18	FAMILY REUNION	O'JAYS

HITS

WAS	IS	TITLE		WKS
1	1	SILLY LOVE SONGS	WINGS	11
3	2	LOVE HANGOVER	DIANA ROSS	6
4	3	GET CLOSER	SEALS & CROFTS	9
6	4	TAKIN IT TO THE STREETS	DOOBIE BROS.	6
2	5	BOOGIE FEVER	SYLVERS	11
7	6	GET UP AND BOOGIE	SIL. CONVENTION	7
9	7	HOT STUFF/FOOL TO CRY	ROLLING STONES	8
8	8	SARA SMILE	HALL & OATES	8
19	9	FRAMED	CHEECH & CHONG	3
5	10	FOOLED AROUND...	E. BISHOP	10
12	11	SHOP AROUND	CAP. & TENNILLE	7
13	12	LOVE IS ALIVE	GARY WRIGHT	6
10	13	WELCOME BACK	JOHN SEBASTIAN	10
11	14	SHANNON	HENRY GROSS	8
20	15	SIXTEEN TONS	DON HARRISON	5
21	16	TAKE THE MONEY AND RUN	STEVE MILLER	4
15	17	DISCO LADY	JOHNNY TAYLOR	13
14	18	HAPPY DAYS	PRATT & MC CLAIN	8
25	19	NEVER GONNA FALL IN LOVE	ERIC CARMEN	3
16	20	SHOW ME THE WAY	PETER FRAMPTON	9
17	21	STRANGE MAGIC	ELO	7
30	22	AFTERNOON DELIGHT	STARLAND VOCAL	2
22	23	DECEMBER 1963	FOUR SEASONS	16
29	24	ROCK AND ROLL MUSIC	BEACH BOYS	2
28	25	CRAZY ON YOU	HEART	2
23	26	LET YOUR LOVE FLOW	BELLAMY BROS.	14
QQ	27	LET 'EM IN	WINGS	1
QQ	28	KISS AND SAY GOODBYE	MANHATTENS	1
QQ	29	YOU'RE MY BEST FRIEND	QUEEN	1
QQ	30	LER HER IN	JOHN TRAVOLTA	1

COMPILED BY Q FOR JUNE 7, 1976

SHOP AROUND

JUST BECAUSE YOU'VE BECOME A YOUNG WOMAN NOW
THERE'S STILL SOME THINGS YOU DON'T UNDERSTAND
BEFORE YOU ASK SOME GUY FOR HIS HAND NOW
KEEP YOUR FREEDOM FOR AS LONG AS YOU CAN NOW
MY MAMA TOLD ME, YOU BETTER SHOP AROUND

THERE'S SOME THINGS THAT I WANT YOU TO KNOW NOW
JUST AS SURE AS THE WIND'S GONNA BLOW NOW
THE MEN'LL COME AND THE MEN ARE GONNA GO NOW
MY MOMMA TOLD ME, YOU BETTER SHOP AROUND

TRY TO GET YOURSELF A BARGAIN GIRL
DON'T YOU BE SOLD ON THE VERY FIRST ONE
GOOD-LOOKING GUYS COME A DIME A DOZEN
TRY TO FIND YOURSELF ONE THAT'S GONNA GIVE
YOU TRUE LOVIN

BEFORE YOU TAKE A MAN AND SAY I DO NOW
MAKE SURE HE'S IN LOVE WITH YOU NOW
MAKE SURE THAT HIS LOVE IS TRUE NOW
I'D HATE TO SEE YOU FEELING SAD AND BLUE NOW
MY MOMMA TOLD ME, YOU BETTER SHOP AROUND

ALBUMS

1.	PETER FRAMPTON	COMES ALIVE
2.	FLEETWOOD MAC	FLEETWOOD MAC
3.	BOZ SCAGGS	SILK DEGREES
4.	SANTANA	AMIGOS
5.	WINGS	AT THE SPEED OF SOUND
6.	ROLLING STONES	BLACK & BLUE
7.	DOOBIE BROTHERS	TAKIN IT TO THE STREETS
8.	LED ZEPPELIN	PRESENCE
9.	QUEEN	NIGHT AT THE OPERA
10.	AEROSMITH	ROCKS
11.	STEELY DAN	THE ROYAL SCAM
12.	AMERICA	HIDEAWAY
13.	ELTON JOHN	HERE & THERE
14.	SEALS & CROFTS	GET CLOSER
15.	JOHNNY TAYLOR	EARGASM

HITS

WAS	IS	TITLE	ARTIST	WKS
2	1	KISS AND SAY GOODBYE	MANHATTANS	7
1	2	AFTERNOON DELIGHT	STARLAND VOCAL BAND	7
4	3	MISTY BLUE	DOROTHY MOORE	4
3	4	MOONLIGHT FEELS RIGHT	STARBUCK	4
8	5	LET 'EM IN	WINGS	7
11	6	BABY I LOVE YOUR WAY	PETER FRAMPTON	5
5	7	FRAMED	CHEECH & CHONG	9
14	8	LET HER IN	JOHN TRAVOLTA	7
6	9	HOT STUFF	ROLLING STONES	14
16	10	TEAR THE ROOF OFF...	PARLIAMENT	3
7	11	LOVE HANGOVER	DIANA ROSS	12
9	12	LOVE IS ALIVE	GARY WRIGHT	12
10	13	TAKE THE MONEY & RUN	STEVE MILLER BAND	10
12	14	SARA SMILE	HALL & OATES	14
19	15	HOLD ON	SONS OF CHAMPLIN	6
18	16	HELL CAT	BELLAMY BROTHERS	6
13	17	TAKIN IT TO THE STREET	DOOBIE BROTHERS	12
17	18	SILLY LOVE SONGS	WINGS	17
23	19	ANOTHER RAINY DAY...	CHICAGO	4
15	20	SHOP AROUND	CAPTAIN & TENNILLE	13
25	21	I NEVER CRY	ALICE Q-PER	4
20	22	GET UP AND BOOGIE	SILVER CONVENTION	13
27	23	GOIN' HOME	AWB	3
28	24	STRUTTIN' MY STUFF	ELVIN BISHOP	2
22	25	ROCK 'N' ROLL MUSIC	BEACH BOYS	8
24	26	GET CLOSER	SEALS AND CROFTS	15
30	27	A LITTLE BIT MORE	DR. HOOK	2
QQ	28	MORE, MORE, MORE	ANREA TRUE	1
QQ	29	STILL THE ONE	ORLEANS	1
QQ	30	DON'T GO BREAKING MY..	ELTON JOHN & KIKI	1

COMPILED BY Q FOR JULY 19, 1976

GET CLOSER

DARLIN' IF YOU WANT ME TO BE CLOSER TO YOU
GET CLOSER TO ME
DARLIN' IF YOU WANT ME TO BE CLOSER TO YOU
GET CLOSER TO ME
DARLIN' IF YOU WANT ME TO LOVE
LOVE ONLY YOU, THEN LOVE ONLY ME
DARLIN' IF YOU WANT ME TO SEE
SEE ONLY YOU , THEN SEE ONLY ME

THERE'S A LINE, I CAN'T CROSS OVER
IT'S NO GOOD FOR ME AND IT'S NO GOOD FOR YOU
AND IT'S NO GOOD FOR YOU
AND THERE'S A FEELIN' DEEP DOWN INSIDE ME
I CAN'T EXPLAIN IT AND YOU'RE WONDERING WHY
YOU SAY WE'VE BEEN LIKE STRANGERS BUT I'M
NOT LIKE THE OTHERS YOU CAN WRAP AROUND
YOURE FINGERS

THERE'S A TIME WHEN I WOULD COME RUNNIN'
I'D DROP EVERYTHING FOR THE TOUCH OF YOUR HAND
IN MINE CAUSE I CAN'T FORGET IT, IT'S LOCKED
IN MY MIND AND I CAN'T GO ON LIVIN'
DAY TO DAY WONDERING IF YOU'LL BE HERE TOMORROW
PEOPLE CHANGE AND YOU'RE CHANGIN'
AND I'VE GIVEN YOU MY ALL THERE'S NO MORE
TO BORROW.

ALBUMS

1.	PETER FRAMPTON	COMES ALIVE
2.	BOZ SCAGGS	SILK DEGREES
3.	WINGS	SPEED OF SOUND
4.	JEFFERSON STARSHIP	SPITFIRE
5.	FLEETWOOD MAC	FLEETWOOD MAC
6.	STEVE MILLER	FLY LIKE AND EAGLE
7.	GORDON LIGHTFOOT	SUMMERTIME DREAM
8.	JEFF BECK	WIRED
9.	GEORGE BENSON	BREEZIN'
10.	AVERAGE WHITE BAND	SOUL SEARCHIN'
11.	NEIL DIAMOND	BEAUTIFUL NOISE
12.	DOOBIE BROTHERS	TAKIN IT...STREETS
13.	CHICAGO	CHICAGO TEN
14.	BEATLES	ROCK 'N' ROLL MUSIC
15.	AEROSMITH	ROCKS

HITS

WAS	IS	TITLE		WKS
1	1	KISS AND SAY GOODBYE	MANHATTANS	8
2	2	AFTERNOON DELIGHT	STARLAND VOCAL	8
6	3	BABY I LOVE YOUR WAY	PETER FRAMPTON	6
5	4	LET 'EM IN	WINGS	8
3	5	MISTY BLUE	DOROTHY MOORE	5
4	6	MOONLIGHT FEELS RIGHT	STARBUCK	5
8	7	LET HER IN	JOHN TRAVOLTA	8
10	8	TEAR THE ROOF OFF	PARLIAMENT	4
15	9	HOLD ON	SONS OF CHAMPLIN	7
9	10	HOT STUFF	STONES	15
11	11	LOVE HANGOVER	DIANA ROSS	13
28	12	MORE, MORE, MORE	ANDREA TRUE	2
12	13	LOVE IS ALIVE	GARY WRIGHT	13
13	14	TAKE THE MONEY & RUN	STEVE MILLER	11
19	15	ANOTHER RAINY DAY...	CHICAGO	5
21	16	I NEVER CRY	ALICE COOPER	5
30	17	DON'T GO BREAKING MY HEART	ELTON & KIKI	2
7	18	FRAMED	CHEECH & CHONG	10
23	19	GOIN HOME	AWB	4
24	20	STRUTTIN' MY STUFF	ELVIN BISHOP	3
14	21	SARA SMILE	HALL & OATES	15
27	22	A LITTLE BIT MORE	DR. HOOK	2
17	23	TAKIN IT TO THE STREETS	DOOBIE BROTHERS	13
18	24	SILLY LOVE SONGS	WINGS	18
29	25	STILL THE ONE	ORLEANS	2
20	26	SHOP AROUND	CAP. & TENNILLE	14
25	27	ROCK 'n' ROLL MUSIC	BEACH BOYS	9
26	28	GET CLOSER	SEALS & CROFTS	16
22	29	GET UP AND BOOGIE	SIL. CONVENTION	14
QQ	30	WITH YOUR LOVE	JEFFERSON STAR.	1

COMPILED BY Q FOR JULY 26, 1976

GET TICKETS FOR KCBQ SEAWORLD NIGHT, JULY 31 – 8 P.M. - 1 A.M., AT BILL GAMBLE'S AND CALIFORNIA FIRST BANK

ALBUMS

1.	PETER FRAMPTON	COMES ALIVE
2.	NEIL DIAMOND	BEAUTIFUL NOISE
3.	JEFFERSON STARSHIP	SPITFIRE
4.	GEORGE BENSON	BREEZIN
5.	BOZ SCAGGS	SILK DEGREES
6.	FLEETWOOD MAC	FLEETWOOD MAC
7.	STEVE MILLER	FLY LIKE AND EAGLE
8.	AWB	SOUL SEARCHIN
9.	WINGS	AT THE SPEED OF SOUND
10.	JEFF BECK	WIRED
11.	DOOBIE BROTHERS	TAKIN IT...STREETS.
12.	STARLAND VOCAL BAND	STARLAND VOCAL BAND
13.	CHICAGO	CHICAGO TEN
14.	GORDON LIGHTFOOT	SUMMERTIME DREAM
15.	HEART	DREAMBOAT ANNIE

2884 University, S.D.

295-8364

TOLL FREE BOOGIE PHONE

Escondido; Vista; Poway; San Marcos; Pauma Valley; Ramona; San Pasqual

747-1133

SAN DIEGO: 570-1234

SAN DIEGO'S FAVORITE ALBUMS

1. WINGS/LONDON TOWN/CAPITOL
2. STEELY DAN/AJA/ABC
3. CHUCK MANGIONE/FEELS SO GOOD/A & M
4. GEORGE BENSON/WEEKEND IN L.A./WB
5. BEE GEES, VARIOUS ARTISTS/SATURDAY NIGHT FEVER/RSO
6. ERIC CLAPTON/SLOWHAND/RSO
7. WARREN ZEVON/EXCITABLE BOY/ELEKTRA
8. KANSAS/POINT OF KNOW RETURN/KIRSHNER/EPIC
9. VAN HALEN/VAN HALEN/WB
10. GENESIS/AND THEN THERE WERE THREE/ATLANTIC
11. HEATWAVE/CENTRAL HEATING/EPIC
12. JEFFERSON STARSHIP/EARTH/GRUNT
13. EARTH, WIND & FIRE/ALL 'N ALL/COLUMBIA
14. JIMMY BUFFETT/SON OF A SON OF A SAILOR/ABC
15. BILLY JOEL/THE STRANGER/COLUMBIA
16. HEART/MAGAZINE/MUSHROOM
17. ATLANTA RHYTHM SECTION/CHAMPAGNE JAM/POLYDOR
18. ROBERTA FLACK/BLUE LIGHTS IN THE BASEMENT/ATLANTIC
19. JACKSON BROWNE/RUNNING ON EMPTY/ASYLUM
20. GERRY RAFFERTY/CITY TO CITY/UNITED ARTISTS

"SHOTGUN TOM" AND JERRY LEWIS URGE YOU TO SPONSOR A "FUN EVENT" FOR THE FIGHT AGAINST MUSCULAR DYSTROPHY.

B-100 fm

SAN DIEGO'S FAVORITE NEW MUSIC!

EVERY KINDA PEOPLE
ROBERT PALMER

TWO TICKETS TO PARADISE
EDDIE MONEY

MISS YOU
ROLLING STONES

USED TA BE MY GIRL
O'JAYS

YOU'RE THE LOVE
SEALS & CROFTS

TAKE A CHANCE ON ME
ABBA

STAY
JACKSON BROWNE

CHEESEBURGER IN PARADISE
JIMMY BUFFETT

SONGS LISTED UNDER 'FAVORITE NEW MUSIC' ARE NOW RECEIVING, OR BEING CONSIDERED FOR, AIRPLAY ON B-100.

THE LISTING OF RECORDS HEREIN IS THE OPINION OF B-100 BASED ON ITS SURVEY OF RECORD SALES AND LISTENER RESPONSE.

SAN DIEGO'S STEREO FAVORITES

VOLUME FOUR/NUMBER TWENTY-THREE June 9, 1978

LAST WEEK	THIS WEEK	SONG TITLE	ARTIST	WEEKS ON
1	1	WITH A LITTLE LUCK	WINGS	11
4	2	Feels So Good	Chuck Mangione	8
3	3	On Broadway	George Benson	8
6	4	Shadow Dancing	Andy Gibb	8
9	5	Baby Hold On	Eddie Money	7
5	6	Deacon Blues	Steely Dan	9
8	7	Imaginary Lover	Atlanta Rhythm Section	10
2	8	Closer I Get To You	Roberta Flack & Donny Hathaway	8
10	9	I Was Only Joking	Rod Stewart	9
7	10	Fantasy	Earth, Wind & Fire	10
16	11	Love Is Like Oxygen	Sweet	6
12	12	Disco Inferno	Trammps	7
14	13	You Belong To Me	Carly Simon	6
11	14	Because The Night	Patti Smith	10
27	15	Baker Street	Gerry Rafferty	4
20	16	This Time I'm In It For Love	Player	5
28	17	Tumbling Dice	Linda Ronstadt	4
13	18	If I Can't Have You	Yvonne Elliman	14
25	19	Still The Same	Bob Seger	5
18	20	Werewolves Of London	Warren Zevon	8
15	21	More Than A Woman	Bee Gees	14
24	22	Heartless	Heart	5
19	23	Dust In The Wind	Kansas	19
17	24	Goodbye Girl	David Gates	11
30	25	Wonderful Tonight	Eric Clapton	4
26	26	It's A Heartache	Bonnie Tyler	4
--	27	Follow You, Follow Me	Genesis	3
29	28	This Magic Moment	Richie Furay	4
--	29	Bluer Than Blue	Michael Johnson	3
--	30	Only The Good Die Young	Billy Joel	3
--	31	Runaway	Jefferson Starship	3

The songs listed herein are arranged in order according to popularity based on listener input to the KBEST 95 Music Department.

KBEST 95 BEST 300 MEMORIAL DAY COLLECTOR EDITION, VOLUME II copyright 1993

Forget the beach.

Hit the streets Memorial Day weekend for La Mesa's

Sunday, May 30 11am-10pm
Monday, May 31 11am-6pm
Downtown La Mesa

Dress in your favorite duds and bring the entire family for non-stop B-Bop Fun including:

- 'The' classic and street rod car show of the year
- Fabulous 50's musical entertainment and dancing to The Mar Dels, The Cat-illacs, Dr. Feelgood and the Interns of Love, Chuck and the Chickens, Sweet Sensations, Cherry Cola and more.
- Make-A-Wish Foundation's Kids Carnival
- Mouth-watering 50's style food served up by Corvette Diner's 'B-Bop Cafe' and many others
- Hula Hoop and costume contests
- **Drawing for a cruise for two to the Mexican Riviera!**

Admission is just $5 per person
Kids under 12 are free!